Planning in the Moment
Two and Three Year Olds

Children are most engaged – and therefore learn best – when they are following their own interests. In this book, Anna Ephgrave shows how her acclaimed 'planning in the moment' approach can be used with two and three year olds with dramatic results for both children and staff. It reveals the impact that free-flowing, child-initiated play has on very young children's well-being, making them feel safe and secure and consequently helping them to be fully engaged in their learning.

The first part of the book clearly explains the principles of child-initiated play and demonstrates how practitioners can create the best possible environment for very young children, also looking at the resources and practices that need to be in place for them to flourish. There is detailed guidance on the role of the practitioner, including how adults should observe children's play before deciding how – or if – to interact in that moment to ensure that each interaction moves learning forward and supports the child's unique development. The second part of the book tracks some of the events from each month in the toddler room of an outstanding preschool, following a cohort of children through a year, to show how the setting moved from topic-based, adult-led activities to a fully child-led way of working.

Key features include:

- Over 350 full-colour photos to illustrate practice
- Specific guidance on using the 'in the moment' approach with all children, including those with additional needs
- Advice on working with parents, individual children and groups
- Examples of individual learning journeys
- Photocopiable templates of 'focus-child' sheets

Covering all aspects of practice from the organisation of the room and outdoor environment to the routines and boundaries that ensure children are safe and happy, this book is essential reading for anyone who works with two and three year olds.

Anna Ephgrave has been teaching for over 27 years. Her most recent post was Assistant Head Teacher responsible for the early years and year one at Carterhatch Infant School, which was graded as Outstanding in its most recent inspection. Anna is now an independent consultant, trainer and author, supporting practitioners both in the United Kingdom and abroad. She has written four highly successful books for Routledge: *Planning in the Moment with Young Children*, *The Reception Year in Action*, *Year One in Action*, and *The Nursery Year in Action*, which was the winner of Nursery World's Professional Books Award, 2017.

Planning in the Moment with Two and Three Year Olds

Child-initiated Play in Action

Anna Ephgrave

Routledge
Taylor & Francis Group

LONDON AND NEW YORK

First published 2020
by Routledge
2 Park Square, Milton Park, Abingdon, Oxon OX14 4RN

and by Routledge
52 Vanderbilt Avenue, New York, NY 10017

Routledge is an imprint of the Taylor & Francis Group, an informa business

British Library Cataloguing-in-Publication Data
A catalogue record for this book is available from the British Library

Library of Congress Cataloging-in-Publication Data
A catalog record for this book has been requested

ISBN: 978-0-367-14014-4 (hbk)
ISBN: 978-0-367-14015-1 (pbk)
ISBN: 978-0-429-02976-9 (ebk)

Typeset in Univers
by Apex CoVantage, LLC

Printed and bound in Great Britain by
TJ International Ltd, Padstow, Cornwall

Contents

Detailed contents

Acknowledgements

I have been working with Staple Hill Stars Pre-school for three years, and the staff have become colleagues and friends. This book would not have been possible without their dedication and hard work. The owners, Helen Clegg and Leanne Ford, welcomed me into their setting with open minds and a passion to develop practice to benefit the children and families at the preschool. They have worked so hard to make changes and to support every member of staff to adapt and develop their individual practice too.

Over the course of the year from September 2018 to July 2019, there were many adults who worked in the toddler room. I would like to thank each of them for their hard work in ensuring that the practice was indeed outstanding. Some were reluctant to be photographed and/or filmed, but eventually they overcame their nerves and carried on in their role – forming trusting relationships with the children and their families and then playing and interacting with the children in the preschool.

So, a massive thank you to Hayley Franklin, Kaz May, Kerry King, Jen Hewitt, Gina James, Anna Clarke, Nicole Hooper, Freya Digby, Monika Chocha and Hazel Liebert.

This book is about the children in the 'toddler room' – the children aged 2–3 – but the whole preschool has adopted the principles described in this book, and I would also like to thank Shaneen Lee, who is the room leader for the 3- to 4-year-olds at Staple Hill.

This book comes alive through the photos of the children, and without these images, the book would not be as vibrant and engaging as it is. I must therefore thank the families for agreeing to allow their children to appear in the book (and in a few cases, the parents too). And finally, as ever, I must thank the children for being children – their curiosity, energy, enthusiasm, creativity and resilience shines through.

Each child is unique, and I must thank the staff for valuing and building on the unique contribution that each child brings. Never a dull moment in the toddler room – and I thank the staff for recognising and exploiting thousands of 'teachable moments' each and every day. The children have had a wonderful year, thanks to your hard work and dedication to your job. You have given them the firmest of foundations which will benefit them throughout their lives. This book gives just a glimpse into what you do every day – such an important and complex job, which you all do with compassion, enthusiasm and energy – quite a remarkable team. Thank you so, so much.

Anna

Introduction

Child-initiated play all day

This book focuses on the toddler provision at Staple Hill Stars Pre-school and covers every aspect of the organisation and outcomes. Although I have written other books, I am often asked to talk specifically about the 2–3 age range and how the idea of *Planning in the Moment* can work with this age. Staple Hill Stars Pre-school has developed their practice over the past three years, moving from topic-based, adult-led activities to purely child-initiated play with planning in the moment. This now means that for almost every moment that they are in the setting, the children have autonomy. These changes have had dramatic results. The children are now making excellent progress – they are happy and engaged, and the behaviour has improved considerably. The atmosphere in the room is now calm and purposeful, and workload for staff has reduced. Having spent so much time at this preschool in Bristol, I thought it was a superb opportunity to document how they went about changing their practice and the impact that this has had on the children and the staff.

Structure of the book

The book is divided into two parts, with the first looking at various aspects of the rationale and practical aspects of the setting. The second part of the book looks at some of the events that occurred during each month in the setting. Readers can obviously 'dip' into any chapter of the book, but this might give a distorted picture. The complexities of running any early years provision are immense, and it is very difficult to simplify or summarise these into a short text. Therefore, it is important to read all chapters if you wish to gain a full understanding of the pedagogy and practicalities that have resulted in this preschool being so successful.

The photo explains the pedagogy

Although it is very difficult to condense the messages of the book, the image at the beginning of this Introduction does actually tell us a great deal about the underlying pedagogy of the preschool. The photo was taken in September, when the children had only been in the setting for about a week. It shows happy, engaged children in an enabling environment, supported by skilful, enthusiastic staff – staff who are free to respond to events as they happen. These children have autonomy – they are 'playing', which is the most powerful vehicle for learning with young children.

Well-being is prioritised

The happiness – or well-being – of the children is the priority, since the staff recognise that without this, the children cannot relax and cannot then engage with the opportunities on offer. Therefore, a large section of Chapter 2 covers this, and in the September diary (Chapter 6) in Part II, there is further discussion about how to support and encourage these high levels of well-being. This work is ongoing throughout the year but must guide everything during the induction and settling periods.

The environment is critical

The photo shows a large section of the outdoor environment and illustrates how the organisation of the resources and the amount and type of resources are critical. If there had not been fabric available, then the adult could not have introduced this activity. In addition, had there not been lots of fabric available, then the children would not have been able to get involved in the way they did. Chapter 3 is devoted to the organisation of the environment, but the results of this are very well illustrated in this photo.

The role of the adults is complex

The role of the adults is clear too. Obviously, they are responsible for organising the environment and for ensuring the well-being of the children. Both these roles are ongoing throughout the year. However, once the children have settled into the preschool, then their role is to "teach" as they interact, at every possible opportunity. This is explored more thoroughly in Chapter 4, but the photo at the beginning of this chapter is an example of this 'teaching'. Thus, Hayley responded to the high winds and the excitement that this created in the children, to introduce them to a new experience – experimenting with lengths of fabric in the windy conditions. Once she had shown them what the wind could do to the fabric, then the children were keen to try this for themselves. Again, the carefully organised environment meant that they could easily access their own pieces of fabric and start experimenting themselves.

Child-initiated play is hugely complex to organise well

What I have described is 'child-initiated play', and although this may sound quite 'simple', it is hugely complex to organise and maintain in a way that does not result in chaos. The 2–3 room at Staple Hill Stars caters for up to 20 children in any one session. If each child is to remain happy (with high levels of well-being) and engaged in play of their own choice, then I hope that anyone reading this will begin to realise just how complex this is. Chapter 2 looks in detail at various aspects of the organisation that need to be considered, discussed and agreed. This includes developing an agreed vision, ensuring every member of the team is 'on board', agreeing expectations around behaviour and the routines of the day and so on. This chapter also includes a section about how the needs of individual children are met, which includes children with additional needs, and this is discussed further in Chapter 4. Chapter 2 also looks at schematic play with children at this age.

Paperwork and record keeping

Another 'layer' of complexity, which is not evident in the photo, is the administration, paperwork and record keeping that has to be in place in any preschool. Chapter 5 considers many aspects of the 'paperwork' of the team. It should be acknowledged that for private settings, there is another layer of responsibility, which includes the requirements to have various policies in place and to ensure that all regulations are complied with. These 'extras' are beyond the scope of this book (which is primarily concerned with practice), but any such requirements are set out in the Early Years Foundation Stage (EYFS). Chapter 5 is mainly explaining how the staff document some of the learning that takes place and how the development of the children is tracked. The preschool has opted to use the Early Excellence Assessment Tracker (EExAT), and there is a section in Chapter 5 which describes this as well.

Planning is done 'in the moment'

The *planning* that is done in this preschool is done 'in the moment'. This is referred to throughout the book and is partly explained in Chapter 4. The adults observe the children, think about what they see and hear, and this then determines how, or if, they interact with the children in that moment. Thus, **the cycle of 'observation, assessment, planning and teaching' is completed hundreds of times each day by each practitioner.** Some of these interactions are recorded on paper afterwards, and this is explained in Chapter 5, with several completed examples included as well.

Amazing events occurred each month

The second part of the book is broken down to explore some of the events that occurred in the preschool in each month.

As you start to read this book, you might be tempted to jump to the examples from each month. However, I would urge you to read the earlier chapters, as these give all the underlying information and explanation of why the preschool is organised in the way that it is. A preschool will not be successful if the team do not have a clear vision, sound reasoning for that vision and a meticulous plan for how that is going to be put into practice. The results of all this discussion, agreement and preparation will lead to the sort of learning that you will see in Part II. However, without a clear vision, reasoning and preparation, the result could be disastrous – so please read the early chapters and then look to see what this can achieve, as exemplified in the second part of the book.

About the author

I have worked with children since the age of 13. I had grown up in the Woodcraft Folk and, at age 13, was running a group for 6- to 10-year-olds. This voluntary work continued for over 30 years. I also had a baby while studying at university and a second baby a couple of years later. When my children were very young, I worked as a child-minder and also ran 'toddler groups' in the local area. I became a teacher 30 years ago and was also a foster carer for ten years whilst teaching. As an assistant head, I was in a school with a children's centre attached and was responsible for the training of staff working with children aged 0–6. Most recently, in the last three years, I have been working voluntarily at Staple Hill Stars Pre-school in Bristol, and it is that setting which is the base for this book. I have also been spending several days each month looking after my granddaughter for the past three years. As this book goes to print, she is turning 3, so I have had the unique opportunity to spend many, many hours observing a child in this pivotal year. Thus, I have experience of children of many ages and in many different situations. I have also read and studied, not only for qualifications, but also out of fascination and, sometimes, frustration when trying to find the best ways to support young children. Everything in my life experiences – personal, voluntary, professional and academic – has led me to conclude that, once they feel secure, **children become most deeply engaged when they have autonomy** – when they are able to choose what to do – when they are initiating their own 'play'.

What is more, nothing in my life has ever demonstrated that this is not true. This applies to children from all backgrounds and all ages; a newborn baby, a toddler, a vulnerable foster child, a child on the autistic spectrum, a child without any English, a year one child, a child who has delayed development, a child who is exceeding typical development or a child with additional needs. This book will focus on children in the 2–3 room, but please bear in mind that the principles and messages apply to all young children. The staff at the preschool share this understanding and passion, and it is this clear rationale and understanding that has led them to develop the practice at the preschool with great success.

PART I

Key principles

1 **Child-initiated play – why?**

As you read this book, you will see that I am suggesting that young children should be having 'child-initiated' play for as much of the time as possible that they are in a setting. This chapter will explain briefly why child-initiated play is so powerful and will also begin to consider how complex it is to organise well. **This is not an easy option.** Anyone who has spent time with one young child at home will realise how powerful their exploratory drive is at this age. It is exhausting to spend time with a 2-year-old – allowing them to lead the play and activity – and all the time keeping them safe, keeping them engaged, coping with their physical needs, coping with the inevitable 'mess'. Imagine if you have 20 or more children in one space, with just one adult to four children and with the added pressure of record keeping, assessment and tracking. For every child to be able to initiate their own play is hugely complex, and the following chapters will explain in greater detail how best to organise this. The chapters will also give some detailed examples of the play that occurred with the 2–3s at Staple Hill Stars. Another strong message in the book is that we must prioritise where we put our effort and time, and this must be based on prioritising those things that will have most impact on the children. You will begin to see that any **paperwork needs to be minimised** so that the staff are free to spend time ensuring the well-being and engagement of the children.

In order to understand why child-initiated play is so important, I am going to give a brief introduction to brain development. When a child's brain develops, they are learning and developing. **It is important to have a simple and clear rationale to explain why we are supporting child-initiated play, and the link to brain development can help with this.**

Brain development

If you ever visit a setting, I would advise that you look at the children. Observe them in the setting. Observe them for quite a while. Observe different children at different times of the session/day and in different areas of the setting. In the best settings, visitors always comment about how 'calm and purposeful' the children are. This is actually a comment about the amount of brain development that is occurring – that is, the amount of learning. It is also a comment about the high **well-being and involvement** of the children. The children are happy (meaning that they feel secure in the setting), and they are engaged (the setting has an environment and staff who are meeting their needs). If you are visiting in the period when children are being settled, then you might see less engagement, because the children have not yet settled and do not yet feel secure and therefore cannot relax and engage with what is on offer.

Throughout this book, whenever I use the word **engaged,** I mean **Level 4 or 5 involvement** as described by Ferre Laevers – see in the next section and in Appendix A.

Ferre Laevers

Level of involvement

Involvement focuses on the extent to which pupils are operating to their full capabilities. In particular it refers to whether the child is focused, engaged and interested in various activities.

The Leuven Scale for Involvement

1 Low activity
   Activity at this level can be simple, stereotypic, repetitive and passive. The child is absent and displays no energy. There is an absence of cognitive demand. The child characteristically may stare into space. NB: This may be a sign of inner concentration.

2 A frequently interrupted activity
   The child is engaged in an activity, but half of the observed period includes moments of non-activity, in which the child is not concentrating and is staring into space. There may be frequent interruptions in the child's concentration, but his/her involvement is not enough to return to the activity.

3 Mainly continuous activity
   The child is busy at an activity, but it is at a routine level, and the real signals for involvement are missing. There is some progress, but energy is lacking and concentration is at a routine level. The child can be easily distracted.

4 Continuous activity with intense moments
   The child's activity has intense moments during which activities at Level 3 can come to have special meaning. Level 4 is reserved for the kind of activity seen in those intense moments, and can be deduced from the 'involvement signals'. This level of activity is resumed after interruptions. Stimuli from the surrounding environment, however attractive, cannot seduce the child away from the activity.

5 Sustained intense activity
   The child shows continuous and intense activity, revealing the greatest involvement. In the observed period, not all the signals for involvement need be there, but the essential ones must be present: concentration,

creativity, energy and persistence. This intensity must be present for almost all the observation period.

Engagement is the key indicator about the quality of any setting – a measure of how much learning is happening at any time. Once a young child has settled, then if the environment is appropriate, they will become engaged.

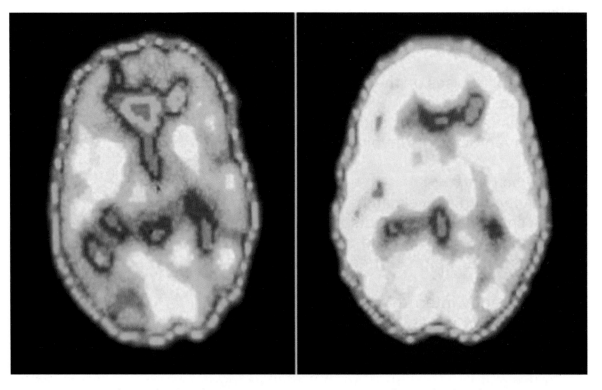

Not engaged–Level 1 involvement   Engaged–Level 5 involvement

We know intuitively that our vision is to get all children **engaged**. Our intuition is justified and now we need to articulate the underlying rationale for this belief:

When children are deeply engaged, their brain is developing and new synapses are forming – that is, they are making progress – they are learning.

We also know that a child who is bored, passive, quiet and not engaged is not making progress – their brain is not growing when they are in that state. We do not need to carry out an experiment to prove this. Brain scans demonstrate this clearly and the long-term effects of low engagement have been demonstrated in the case of the Romanian orphans who were born in the '70s and '80s.

We must also recognise and believe that every child wants to be engaged. If we have children who are not engaged, we cannot blame them. We must look to see what we can do to engage them. The work of Professor Ferre Laevers is complimented by the work of Bowlby and supports the approach and beliefs that I observe in practitioners all over the world. Bowlby was one of the first people to write about attachment theory, and his ideas have been adapted and developed by numerous psychologists and authors since. These theories can be presented in various ways, but in simple terms, babies need to form trusting relationships at a young age. This then allows them to be in a 'secure' state in which their natural desire to learn and develop can be optimised. Anything which disrupts this state will alter the chemical make-up in the brain and hinder development. Thus, the developmentally inappropriate practice of formalised, adult-led learning that is being imposed on so many young children is actually preventing the very development that these practices are supposed to promote. In some settings that cater for 2-year-olds, they are being treated in the same way as much older children. It is always preferable to observe the child in front of you, assess what they need in that moment and respond to them in a developmentally appropriate way.

Levels of involvement

Ferre Laevers has developed descriptors for various levels of involvement, and these can be used as a simple, objective way of measuring the engagement of an individual, group or class. The descriptors are given above and in Appendix A. I have often shown these to external inspectors and their response is that Level 5 (with concentration, creativity, energy and persistence) is equivalent to an 'outstanding' grade.

There are many ways in which these levels of involvement can be used:

Individual children

As mentioned earlier, we start with the assumption that all children want to be engaged, that is, they want to be at Level 5. In a superb setting, if a child is not becoming engaged, then the descriptors can be used to monitor a child throughout a day or a week at regular intervals in order to uncover patterns or preferences. Always bear in mind with such a child that there might be external factors causing emotional well-being to be affected, and remember that a child with poor emotional well-being is not able to become deeply engaged. However, such monitoring can be a powerful way to see which sessions or events do engage a child and which clearly do not. Starting with the assumption that they do want to be engaged, it is then possible to see which types of session are 'working' for the particular child. For the very young children that we are focussing on in this book, (and indeed for children of any age), it might also reveal when they are tired, hungry, thirsty etc. – and again, we know that children cannot engage in learning if their basic physical needs have not been met.

Groups

The same descriptors can be used to assess the quality of play when children are playing in groups. In the rooms that cater for children aged 24 months up to potentially 47 months, there will be many children who play alongside others, but there will be some who play *with* others. The descriptors can be used to gauge the level of involvement of small groups of children who are playing together and also for the room as a whole.

The levels can also be used to consider the effectiveness (or indeed the appropriateness) of adult-led group sessions. Again, assuming that we are aiming to deliver practice that will see most children at Level 4 or 5, we can quickly start to see which sessions or events are appropriate and productive in terms of engagement/involvement (and therefore progress). For example, if we are delivering an input on the carpet, then we should have the level descriptors in mind. When the children start to fidget and become distracted, then this tells us that the session has become unproductive. It does not tell us that the children are 'naughty' or that 'they can't concentrate' or that 'they have ADHD'. It tells us that what we are offering is not engaging and therefore is not supporting synapse formation and learning. Once we accept this, it is clear that group sessions in the 2–3 room are rarely appropriate. If you do have the children gathered at any time (perhaps just before lunch, or just before they go home), then the more interactive the session can be, the better.

I'd also urge practitioners to use these levels to measure the effectiveness of focussed tasks, snack time, circle time etc. In all these cases, the level of involvement is often very low, the adults and children can become quite stressed and the learning is minimal. It is, then, a very useful tool for practitioners to use as a way of assessing and then developing a change in the practice.

Environment

The levels can also be used to see which areas of an environment are 'working', which areas are delivering good levels of involvement and which are not. This is an on-going process, but some areas are always engaging and others are rarely so. Also, it will help practitioners see which areas are rarely, if ever, used. Such areas obviously need to be changed, as they are essentially a 'wasted space'. Chapter 3 on environment will give detailed information and ideas that can support the development of an environment that is engaging.

Resources

I would recommend using the levels as a way of assessing the effectiveness of resources. Whether there is a huge budget or not, it is best to have mainly resources which are open-ended and can therefore be used in many different ways. For example, for small world play, rather than having a pirate ship, a doll's house, a castle, a rocket, a caravan, a farm and a car park for the children to use, there is far more potential for engagement with wooden blocks, Duplo, pieces of fabric, paper and pens etc. In this way, the children can create their own rocket, car park, castle etc. Again, further details can be found in Chapter 3 on environment.

So how do we achieve the best levels of involvement (and thus ensure maximum progress)?

As explained in the introduction, all my life experiences in numerous capacities, working with young children, have convinced me that the best levels of involvement (leading to the best progress) are achieved when children's well-being is high and we then let them choose what to do – when they have autonomy. This has become known as 'free-flow play', 'child-initiated play', 'choosing time', 'explore and learn time', 'continuous provision', etc. But let's be clear – within agreed boundaries – I am talking about children **playing** where they want, with whatever they choose, for as long as they want, in whatever way they want.

This sounds simple, but if every child in a setting is to be able to play as they choose then there are several things that need to be in place to support this:

- A **prioritisation of well-being** above all else, recognising that high well-being is critical in order for a child to feel secure, which in turn will allow them to become involved.
- Ensuring that **physical needs have been met** – hunger, thirst, temperature, sleep.
- **Consistent boundaries, expectations and routines** (within which each child can then relax and have the freedom that they need in order to learn effectively.)
- **An enabling environment** (which is organised to meet the ever-changing needs and interests of each unique child). This book will be of interest to people working from home and also in various settings. Therefore, the words 'room', 'class', 'setting' etc. should be read as meaning the 'space' where the children are.
- **Skilful, empathic adults interacting appropriately** to form warm relationships and to support each child in a way that respects them, preserves their autonomy and offers genuine interest and fascination. Throughout this book, I use the words 'adult', 'practitioner', 'teacher', but these all refer to any adult who is responsible for a child.
- **Manageable systems of assessment and record keeping** (to satisfy any statutory requirements without impeding the progress of the children and while protecting the well-being of the staff).

These things are dealt with in the following chapters, and each is critical if the **play** is to be successful and productive. What is **not necessary** are any written forward plans. If the children have genuine choice, if it is genuinely child-initiated play, then **we do not know what the children will choose** to do and **we cannot, therefore, pre-plan the activities or the learning outcomes**.

So the simple message is that:-

- High quality child-initiated play results in deep involvement
- Deep involvement indicates brain development and learning
- **Therefore, child-initiated play results in learning**

2 What needs to be in place?

Hayley is a member of staff at Staple Hill Stars, and I asked her about how the 2–3 room used to be run and how the children responded.

"The sessions were very structured, with a complicated timetable and routines throughout the day.

"Everyone would arrive, and they would have to stay indoors and sit down on the carpet for the welcome song, and a chat about the weather and so on. We would then offer the children one of our 'time-consuming' activities – 'occupying activities', I suppose. This would include colouring sheets, painting, a sensory play activity and so on. Or they could explore other areas indoors – but all the activities in the other areas had been pre-planned too. So, for example, if our topic was the farm, then every area was set up around the topic – so there would be farm animals in the sand, a craft activity to do with the farm, the toy farm was put out, along with other 'toys' relating to the farm etc. I used to spend my weekends sourcing stuff, thinking up activities, cutting out templates and so on. These were then used for a week only. After an hour of this indoors, it was tidy up time, and then all the children would sit and have snack around tables. Each child brought in their own snack pot which had been prepared at home.

"After snack, we had one hour outdoors. So everyone had to get their coat and boots on and everyone went outside. In the garden we had a few bikes, a tiny sand pit and some balls and hoops. Then we would all come back in for story and singing, which was about half an hour, and then it was lunch time or home time.

"The afternoon was exactly the same – the same activities were re-set indoors, ready for the afternoon session.

"The children were bored, the behaviour was on another level, the children were constantly being told to stop doing things and directed to do other things that they weren't interested in.

"When I think back to my role at that time – it felt like being a farmer, herding the children – 'We must go to this area and now we must go to this area'. I was constantly having to manage behaviour – fighting, arguing etc. – behaviour was a big problem. We also had to run some intervention groups when someone used to take children out for speech groups to do activities like 'What's in the box?' It is unbelievable really – how much my role has changed and how much the behaviour of the children has changed."

I then asked Hayley what changes had had the most impact and why she felt this was the case.

"I think that allowing the children to free-flow with no interruptions and less transitions has made the biggest difference. The staff used to be very stressed – getting all the children to go out or in and so on and getting them all to have snack at the same time and ensuring they all completed certain activities. The children were often fighting and arguing while they were waiting for everyone to be gathered or when they didn't want to be at a certain activity at a certain time.

"The children are no longer expected to wait, and even the new children settled far more easily. The children can be in garden as soon as they arrive, and then they can say goodbye to their parent from there and they can watch their parent leave. But they are happy because they are outdoors (or indoors) wherever they are happy to be.

"Enclosing the carpet area has also had major impact. Although the carpet now looks like it has less space, in fact there is less space to run but more room to play calmly. They used to run across the carpet area, and so play was disrupted all the time. In general there are more 'pocketed' areas now, so children enter these and can focus on their play.

"We also changed so many resources, and this has had a huge impact too. When we were doing topics, we would change the resources every week. At the beginning of this process of change, I didn't want to listen to the idea of reducing the amount of resources. I was quite adamant saying things like, 'They love that buzzy light-up aeroplane' and the farm, rocket, zoo and so on. I wanted to keep these things. I couldn't understand how the children would be engaged if we didn't change the resources each week, and I also worried that they would miss these familiar 'toys'. I used to plan the following week every Sunday. Everything was planned – so even though the water, sand and play dough were part of the continuous provision – even in these areas, we changed what was in there – for example, farm cutters in the play dough and so on. We would also rotate the construction toys, so, for example, Duplo one week, then stickle bricks the next week.

"After the changes were made, I was quickly convinced – it is the easiest answer – give them less choice – but support them to use their imaginations by providing more natural, open-ended resources which are available and accessible all the time.

"We are also less 'scared' now, for example with scissors – we never let them have scissors before. But now we give them trust and responsibility – we have high expectations and they rise to this.

"The role of the adult has had to change a lot. We are no longer 'farmers herding the children around'. Our role now is to watch, observe and then extend and build on their interest. Of course, we still supervise and keep them safe, but **now we teach** too. We did 'teach' before, but I used to teach them stuff they didn't want to know, but now I teach them important stuff – in the moment – whatever they are interested in, for example about the wind, the rain, food, tools, building, friends, feelings, stories, independence and so on.

"You have to have all the team on board and everyone has to follow up on the expectations – for example, a few children wanted to be in control, but the staff were calm and consistent, and now all the children understand the expectations and comply. If even one member of staff is not on board, then that can make things fall apart. So consistency from all staff is key. I would like to say to everyone 'When you come to work – give it everything! Be passionate.'

"We no longer do intervention groups, and so the 1–1 support staff come in and shadow the children, bringing any 'teaching strategies' to the child in their play. They can then also help them to socialise with their peers, and so it stops them from missing out, it takes away the barriers to their learning. These adults are now teaching at the same time – so for example if there are words that they wish to introduce, they can do this alongside the child in their play – for example, teaching the word 'cup', they can do this as a child picks up a cup and they can do this with Makaton, the object and the speech. The impact is far greater because the child can stay where they are happy and relaxed and the teaching is in a meaningful situation for the child."

I asked Hayley about how the changes had impacted on the children.

"Those children who need freedom, a relaxed atmosphere, some boys who don't want to sit still or don't want to sit and learn; they now have that space and choice to be outside. Some children learn better outside, and those who want to be inside, they can be inside. All the children can now move about and learn where and how they want. It was always so structured before and like work stations – whereas now the learning is everywhere.

"So for example with language: before, when we had planned activities, you would spend the majority of the time talking at the children – all the time really – and a limited amount of words were 'thrown' at them. Whereas now – it's about prioritising where they are happy and settled, and then adults are modelling language all the time. You start very simply, according to each child, so it might be with turn-taking, getting them to say please and thank you, or it might be words to do with what they are playing with at the time.

"Because the children are content and relaxed, then they are open to the environment and learning. If a child doesn't want to be learning about that topic, then they won't learn. So we are modelling in the moment – we don't ever repeat the wrong word, and we don't tell them 'No!' so there is no pressure – we are relaxed, we wait – and then the speech does develop. So the adults need to be sensitive, and happy too, and keeping their well-being is most important. If the adults are stressed – this can deflate a child very quickly."

These are very powerful words because they come from a practitioner who has been on this journey to change the practice in their setting. Hayley is clearly a reflective practitioner too, willing to trial a new approach (even though she had some initial doubts) and then also willing to admit that her doubts were unfounded. Hayley, along with all members of the team, are fully 'on board' with the new child-led approach, and the children are reaping the benefits.

In the second part of this chapter, I would like to go over some of the points made by Hayley but also to discuss other aspects of practice that are vitally important when working with children aged 2–3 years of age.

Trusting relationships, transitions and induction

If a child has low-level well-being, they will not be able to engage, no matter how superb the setting is. Well-being is built on a foundation of trusting relationships. It is beyond the scope of this book to examine all the possible situations that could mean that a child has not built up trusting relationships from birth. However, practitioners should keep in mind that without good well-being, a child cannot become engaged and deeply involved in learning. No matter how wonderful a home has been, a young child will still need time and empathy to build relationships with the new adults they encounter (in a setting) and to understand the new routines and expectations. Transitions and induction are therefore critical.

When a child sets off for their first day at a new setting, they should be full of positive emotions – excitement, confidence and happiness. This happens if they know exactly where they are going, who will be there, what they will be able to do when they get there and how long they will be staying there. A successful transition means the child settles quickly – meaning that they have good emotional well-being so that they can relax and play immediately – thus learning and developing from day one. Practitioners then greet happy children (who they already know very well), and these children are settled, confident and thus able to learn.

This book is aimed primarily at settings working with children aged 2–3, but the transition procedures are absolutely critical for every child, no matter what age. It is during this period that practitioners can start to build a relationship with the child and the family. Some ideas are as follows (again, as appropriate for the age that you work with):

- Visit the setting that the child is currently attending (if applicable).
- Organise play sessions/visits at your setting (for parent and child).
- Home visit each family and get a family photo.
- Use all information to inform your interactions with the child.
- Plan the induction period meticulously (see the following section).

The **induction/settling period** is critical, must be planned carefully and should take as long as needed for the child to feel secure and relaxed. The main message is to invest as much time as necessary in the settling period and involve the parents as much as possible to 'teach' their own child how to 'be' in the setting. You can even give parents a little 'prompt' card with a list of things to do with their child while they are settling them (**as appropriate for their age**). For example:

- Remind your child about the lovely adults in the setting (and their names).
- Show your child how to self-register.
- Teach your child how to take off their coat and hang it on their peg.
- Show your child the toilets and make sure they can use them independently (if appropriate).
- Show your child around the setting and explain to your child that they can play indoors or outside.
- Explain that they can play with anything, but when they have finished they must put the things away.
- Play with your child and show them how to use the resources.
- Ensure that your child walks indoors and uses a quiet voice indoors.

Some parents find it reassuring to have little tasks such as this to do. It is also a good opportunity to observe how parents interact with their children.

If the practice is superb and a child is still not becoming engaged, then this usually means that there is an **issue with well-being**, possibly related to events at home or in the past. The child might have an attachment disorder, be suffering from the effects of trauma or be living in a volatile home situation. As stated earlier, it is beyond the scope of this book to go into details about the numerous situations which might lead to poor well-being. However, it is our responsibility to ensure that it is not the practice that is stopping the engagement, and then we can seek external support and plan how to address issues that are outside of the setting.

The aim should be that, by the time a child is left by their parent, the staff have built a relationship with the child and their family, and the child is already familiar with the setting. When successful, most children then settle quickly once the parents do eventually leave. Some children (whatever age) may need a parent with them for several weeks, and staff should accommodate this for as long as necessary. Sometimes, after a few sessions, I would encourage a parent to stay in the room, but to just sit and read. This allows the child to relax in the knowledge that their parent is nearby. They are then more likely to have a positive experience and will want to be there even if their parent is not. The most important aspect of the decision about when a parent can leave is that it is made jointly with the parents and also that the child is aware of what is happening.

Key person systems

For younger children and babies, the practitioner that carries out the home visit and who spends time settling a new child should be the key person for that child.

There is a legal requirement in England for each child to have a key person, but there is no stipulation about how a setting organises this. For the youngest children, it is vital that they have a familiar key person who they can form an attachment to. Indeed, advances in the understanding of attachment theory and attachment disorders underpin this piece of legislation. In brief, a baby who receives responsive care and attention from their main carer will develop a good attachment and relationship to that carer. As they grow older, they will be able to form successful relationships with others. Conversely, if a baby receives inadequate or inconsistent care and attention they can develop an attachment disorder, and one of the main outcomes of this is an inability to form relationships as they grow older. For children who could be as young as 24 months in a toddler room, it is vital that they form a strong bond with their key person, as it is within this relationship that they can then relax and explore the environment. It is also important that the children do not become totally reliant on one adult, as this can cause obvious issues if that adult is absent or on a break. Therefore, once the bond is strong with one key person, others should be introduced, and they too should begin to form a relationship with the child. A co-key person system is successful, or a shared responsibility within a room can also work well and avoid unnecessary distress if one adult is absent.

Get transition right, and you will reap the benefits for the whole year. You will have a group of children who are deeply engaged in their learning because they are with adults who know and understand them in an enabling environment that meets their needs and interests. It is definitely worth investing time and energy in this vital aspect of our work.

In the next chapter, I will explore what the environment needs to be like to support the engagement of the children. Obviously, without a **superb environment**, the children will not have anything to do and so will not become engaged, and this can lead to behaviour issues with children who are bored and looking for challenges. Hayley touched on this in her comments earlier, and further details about this are covered in depth in Chapter 3.

Timetables and interruptions

Even with good well-being and a superb environment, one of the main aspects of practice that causes stress and tension is the *timetable* and, in particular, *interruptions*. Again, Hayley explained how the structure of the day has changed at Staple Hill Stars, and I would like to reiterate just how important this is. Imagine you have just started to read a new novel, and ten minutes later you are called away to do something else. You would feel annoyed and frustrated. Imagine if this happens every time you try to read the novel. You will soon give up. It is the same for children. The interruption causes them to become annoyed and frustrated, feelings which they might express through their behaviour. In addition, as they get older, if such interruptions occur regularly, then they will learn that it is not worth investing in their chosen play because they will not be able to see it through to a satisfactory conclusion. When this happens, the children start to opt for simpler, less meaningful play which is easier to leave. This sort of play does not deliver Level 5 involvement; that is, it does not involve creativity, concentration, energy or persistence. Rather, it will be mundane and routine – play that can be left at any moment.

My plea, therefore, is that you consider very carefully any interruptions that you impose on the children's play and ask if they are essential. Any interruptions that cannot be avoided should be moved to the beginning or end of the day or session.

For example, in a room for 2-year-olds, and in many preschool settings, the children might be stopped for a welcome song, key group time, snack time, focussed tasks and circle time. Each interruption causes the children to stop what they are doing (and this is often play in which they are demonstrating great concentration) and to move to a different area of the setting. Moving several 2-year-olds at any one time is very stressful for staff and very frustrating for the children – so why do this? Each key person can greet the children as they arrive; they can play alongside them in their chosen play; snacks can be available for the children to have when they want them and focussed tasks and circle time can be removed altogether, as they are developmentally not appropriate for such young children. Two-year-olds want to be on the move, and then they collapse for a rest. Then they want to be on the move again. Try to allow this natural cycle to happen for each child. Stress, frustration and behaviour issues will reduce immediately.

With fewer interruptions, the levels of involvement will increase, and behaviour will improve. In addition, for some children, the restriction of staying indoors will cause them anxiety and stress. Therefore, if *the doors can be open all day*, then this will again improve engagement and behaviour. Many children can only get to Level 5 involvement outdoors, and there is also much more talking outdoors, so try to have the outdoor area available at all times.

At Staple Hill Stars, the children arrive, self-register and play (indoors or outdoors as they choose). **There are no focussed activities.** This means that when the children are playing, the adults are with them, interacting with them and 'teaching' them whenever they see an opportunity to do so. (See Chapter 4 for further details about this.) Once adults are free from focussed tasks, they are available not only to interact and teach but also to monitor and scan the setting for any potential behaviour issues. They can then deal with these immediately and appropriately – often taking the time to use such opportunities to **'teach' the children the self-regulation skills** that will support their independence in the future.

It is important to note here that 2-year-olds do not like to share. In an ideal world, they would be at home with a caring parent and, in such a situation, they would not be required to share very often. In this respect, it is very stressful for a 2-year-old to be in a setting with so many other 2-year-olds, and this has huge implications on resourcing. In a reception class, you might have one dustpan and brush, and the children will manage to take turns, whereas in the 2–3 room, you might decide to have three dustpans and brushes in order to reduce the arguments. As seen in the photo here, there are enough blocks for both children to play – thus avoiding the need to 'share' in the same way. Playing alongside each other without argument is quite an achievement for any 2-year-old, and sufficient quantities of resources will mean this is more likely to be possible.

Firm and consistent rules

As stated previously, if all the children are engaged in play of their own choice, then behaviour issues are often minimal. However, **it is still essential to have firm, consistent rules** within which the children can relax and have the freedom to play as they wish. Such rules should be kept to a minimum and should be appropriate to the age of the children in the setting. Every member of the staff team should know what the rules are and should be able to ensure they are adhered to without the need to raise a voice. A calm, confident, serious tone is often enough to gain compliance. No adult has the right to shout at a young child.

For children aged 2 or above, then a few simple rules might be:

- When we have finished with something, we put it away.
- Indoors, we walk and we use quiet voices.
- No one touches anyone when we are climbing.

Other rules might be added relating to aprons, coats in the rain etc., but these need to be agreed with the staff team.

Once the rules are agreed, then everyone has to firmly and calmly ensure that they are followed. For example, if a child drops an apron on the floor, instead of replacing it on the hook, then an adult should remind them, saying "**First** put the apron away and **then** you can go". Once this has been stated, it must be followed through, so choose your battles. It might take an hour for the child to pick the apron up, so make sure you have the time to invest. This is, in fact, exactly what happened to me very recently. Many practitioners worry that this type of event will mean that the children will be unhappy. Actually, the reverse is true. The child in this example was from quite a chaotic home where rules and boundaries were inconsistent and where the children had tantrums to get their own way. This child did eventually pick up the apron, I thanked him and he went off to play. The next day, he ran up to me and gave me a hug. He also tidied up happily from then on in the preschool. My ten years as a foster carer taught me that children are testing the boundaries but that they actually want them to remain secure. It is within such boundaries that they can relax, knowing that the adults are in charge and can be trusted (i.e. they mean what they say), and the child can then get on with being the child.

It is also preferable to deal with any such behaviour issues immediately and in a way that relates to the behaviour rather than with reward or sanction systems etc. In the previous example, the child missed out on playing for a while and therefore decided not to do this again. If a child has scribbled on a table, make sure they clean it off. If a child is running or shouting indoors, then take them outside. If a child is silly with the hammer at the woodwork bench, then they are not allowed to have a turn for a set amount of time. If a child has hurt another child, make sure they look at the other child; an adult can verbalise the feelings of the other child, and make sure the child realises how upset you are too. There is little to be gained by making a child say 'sorry'. It is far more important that they begin to feel some empathy for the child who is hurt and to learn a different way to act next time (using words). So any consequence should relate to the behaviour.

Also, extrinsic rewards should not play any part in an early years setting. Children are hardwired to learn, intrinsically motivated to explore and discover, determined to be engaged; they do not need stickers or reward charts for this – they need an enabling environment and skilful staff. A baby who struggles to crawl to reach their favourite toy is rewarded by getting the toy; a child who is trying to master the two-wheeler bike is rewarded by their eventual success – they do not need any other reward. Any praise you do give should be around the process rather than the end result – so praise perseverance, good ideas, initiative, etc. The work around growth mindset is relevant here. It has been shown that children who are told they are 'clever' will in fact give up more easily when things get a bit difficult, whereas children who have been praised for perseverance will just keep trying when things get difficult. So **ban the word 'clever' from your vocabulary!**

As mentioned in Chapter 1, levels of involvement can be used to assess the value of sessions, and once you start to use this, you will see that **group times often deliver low levels of involvement**. This indicates that they are of little value in terms of brain development, that is, learning and progress. These sessions often result in children displaying poor behaviour and getting into 'trouble' because they cannot 'sit still'. The simple solution to this behaviour issue is to **stop the group time** – and this is certainly true for children in the 2–3 room. Whatever you do, **you must not blame the children**. If they are not engaged, they are sending you a clear message; they are saying "This is not how I want to learn. This is not engaging for me. This is a waste of my time." It is very easy to blame the children when, in fact, it is the practice that is inappropriate and needs to be changed. 'Group time' in the 2–3 provision at Staple Hill happens spontaneously – when a child asks for a book to be read, when a child starts to sing, when a child notices something and other children become interested, or (as seen in the following photo) when one child starts a dancing game and others join in.

One other potential cause for lack of engagement is that **young children have not had opportunities to play at home**. Many very young children and even babies now spend **several hours in front of screens**, thus lacking opportunities for movement, interaction, speech, empathy and social skills. They can spend hours in isolation, immobile and silent. This can impact on their ability to talk, play, move and socialise. Practitioners need to take this into account during the induction period and beyond. These children will need far longer time spent on these skills. In particular, they will need to be 'taught' how to play – they will not know what to do with blocks, sand, water, play dough and so on. They may never have had the chance to draw, paint and use scissors. However, once introduced to such experiences, they will quickly become engaged and enthralled by these opportunities.

Your setting is the intervention

With increasing numbers of children entering settings with delayed development, particularly in speech, physical and social skills, it is becoming more common to see intervention groups occurring for younger and younger children. My message is that in the early years **your setting is the intervention**. A child should not be removed to a group in order that their needs can be met. In the best setting, the provision will meet the needs of all the children. Any extra funding, (or extra adults) should be used within the main provision to *bring the intervention to the child*. Thus, a speech therapist should join a child in the sand to promote speech, a physiotherapist should use the outdoor area to support gross motor development and social skills are most powerful when taught 'in the moment' in a real-life situation. Again, further examples of this are given in Chapter 4.

Schemas – Helen Clegg

Helen is one of the owners of Staple Hill Stars. She is a qualified teacher and was a SENCO in a mainstream primary school for ten years. She has extensive knowledge and understanding of the needs of young children and has developed an understanding and appreciation of schematic play that is seen in the toddler room. In the remainder of this chapter, she gives a brief outline of her approach to schematic play and how the preschool has adapted to support and develop this vital aspect of child development.

Again, again, again

Embracing schematic play in toddlers

A typical scene in a toddler room: one child is filling a pram with loose parts and then dumping them all over the room; there are bags filled with 'treasures' (often including the missing puzzle piece); an adult is supporting a child to find suitable items to launch across the room; a child is wearing every accessory and bag at the same time; several visuals and pictures are missing (having been posted in between the gaps in the heaters); and the list could go on. These normal occurrences are when our little scientists are making sense of the world. They are testing out theories, adapting their approach and testing them again. A useful analogy (suggested by Suzanne Zeedyk) is to imagine walking through a field covered in grass. If you walked down the same path again the grass would be slightly flattened. If you continued to walk down the same path you would eventually wear away the grass and create your own pathway. Schemas are a child's tool to learn. They are a practical way, through play, that a child can practise a skill/concept/idea and commit it to memory and create new synapses/pathways in their brains. These can then be accessed throughout their lives when predicting what might happen next: patterns, movements, changes, shape and space, logic, order, sequencing etc.

You may find fascinating children who are fixated on one schema for a long duration of time and who then may move onto another schema, almost working through them in a sequence, or you may get children who apply lots of different schema and sometimes combine schemas together – anything goes in the world of schema! The one thing to remember is that schemas are essential building blocks. What may appear to be a repetitive low-level activity to an adult is actually highly engaging and informative to a young scientist.

So what can we do to support schemas?

A good starting point is to be aware of the main types of schemas:

Transforming

What to look for:
Combining and mixing materials
Putting play dough in the water/sand tray/anywhere it shouldn't be
Mixing paint
Dressing up

What are the children learning?
Cause and effect

What should I provide in the environment?
Baking/dough-making equipment, dressing up clothes, liquid/powder paints, bubbles, containers and tools to mix and whisk

Enveloping

What to look for:
Hiding toys
Covering themselves in paint
Filling up containers till they overflow
Burying things in the sand
Wrapping items with fabric
Putting things in boxes/bags

What are the children learning?
Space and capacity, object permanence

What should I provide in the environment?
Fabric of different sizes, paper, masking and sticky tape, sand, boxes
and bags of different sizes, wet and dry sand, paint, water play

Enclosing

What to look for:
Posting things down the back of the radiator
Den making
Sticking fingers in holes
Hiding

What are the children learning?

Size, shape, measurement and volume

What should I provide in the environment?

Hiding places, large/small boxes, den making equipment, stacking toys, segmented boxes or trays, block play, fences for small world play, tubes and tunnels

Connecting and disconnecting

What to look for:
Undoing clips and redoing
Taking things apart
Undoing and redoing Velcro shoes

What are the children learning?
Joining and separating with different materials

What should I provide in the environment?
Train track, construction toys, masking and sticky tape, string, glue, jig-saw puzzles, magnetic toys, clothes pegs, elastic bands

Positional

What to look for:
Lining up toys
Lays under/stands on tables/blocks/chairs
Favourite peg/seat/spot on the lunchbox trolley

What are the children learning?
Perspective, logic, order, sequencing, classification, symmetry

What should I provide in the environment?
Peg boards, threading, groups of items, e.g. mummy, daddy, baby, train track, vehicles

Rotation

What to look for:
Fiddles with dials and nobs
Turns on taps
Spinning round
Watching washing machines
Plays with wheels on buggies or bikes

What are the children learning?
How things move, spin and turn, shape

What should I provide in the environment?
Wheeled toys, water/sand, wheels, ribbons on sticks, bottles/jars with screw lids

Orientation

What to look for:
  Rocking on a chair
  Hanging upside down
  Running up a slide

What are the children learning?
  Balance, width, weight and height

What should I provide in the environment?
  Slide, climbing equipment, monkey bars, planks of wood with wooden blocks, hanging rings

Trajectory

What to look for:
Jumping off objects
Throwing anything and everything
Pulleys and string

What are the children learning?
Gravity, distance, force, movement

What should I provide in the environment?
Bean bags, balls of all different sizes, balloons, chiffon scarves for indoor throwing, bubbles, paper planes, kites, ramps and tubes, guttering, catapults

Transporting

What to look for:
Carrying objects
Moving objects in bags/wheeled toys/trolleys
Taking resources from one area to another
Making collections of objects

What are the children learning?
Positional language, special awareness, weight, capacity, problem solving

What should I provide in the environment?
Lots of different containers: bags/buckets/baskets/purses/scoops; wheeled toys: bikes/trolleys/diggers/wheelbarrows; buckets on pulleys

This list is not exhaustive, and as a team we often create our own schema names, for example the 'hanging up schema' for the child who frequently likes to hang up their own and other children's coats; the 'red schema' for the child who only wants red things – red cup, red plate, red paint etc.; the 'visual schema' for the child who likes to change how things appear – coloured some particular hue, blindfolds, tubes, telescopes, kaleidoscopes. The more you look the more you find in the fascinating world of schema.

The second is to be aware when children are involved in schematic play. This may be fleeting – tipping up a basket of toys and moving away – or may be a longer task – repeatedly filling and emptying containers in the sand.

The third is to make sure that your toddler room environment provides opportunities for the main schemas.

The fourth is to respond, evaluate and change the environment to promote schematic play if necessary. For example, if you find many toddlers in the trajectory schema, how is this managed and supported in order to be a safe activity? Are there a range of safe, soft objects to be launched? Have the children got free-flow access to outside in order to practise this schema in a larger environment? Are we providing enough resources and risk, especially outside, so that toddlers don't feel the need to practise this schema by jumping off the classroom sofa, or if this is happening, can they be redirected to more suitable climbing resources?

The role of the adult

Taking a phrase from Julie Fisher (2018), it requires careful balancing to "interact and not interfere" when young children are performing schema exploration. Most of the time, children will be totally engrossed in their own awe and wonder.

Occasionally the adult may need to facilitate to avoid too much frustration (it is important to allow the child to persevere and challenge themselves first, only supporting to co-regulate the emotional response to potential frustration). The adult can also provide a dialogue and model language, but this must be done sensitively. Too much speech could distract from the task in hand. The adult should always take time to watch and listen in order to discover what the child has in mind. The adult should always try to follow the child's interests and leads and get involved in the child's suggestions, concept and ideas. Suggestions could be made tentatively but not at the expense of the child's ideas and vision.

Above all, as an adult it is most important to watch, support and encourage schematic play. Once you start to identify examples of this it becomes truly fascinating. You may even identify adults displaying certain schemas wrapping themselves in a duvet; enjoying the movements of rollercoasters or swinging back on chairs; sorting items in categories, folding pieces of paper and other materials into the smallest of squares etc. It is also especially apparent in adults and children when there is neurological deterioration, such as dementia or Batten's disease. It is amazing how heavily schemas feature throughout our lives.

You might like to study the following photo and see how many 'schemas' are in evidence.

(Helen Clegg – Owner Staple Hill Stars Pre-school)

To summarise: If we want children at Level 5 involvement for as much time as possible, then several aspects of practice must be reviewed and developed as necessary. Settings who cater for children aged 2–3 must ensure that:-

- Children have formed a trusting relationship with practitioners
- Induction is carefully planned and involves parents as much as possible
- Children have 'settled' and feel secure and confident in the environment
- The environment is superb (see Chapter 3)
- Children have long periods of uninterrupted free-flow play
- Adults are free to interact with children as they play
- There are a few rules, calmly and consistently enforced

- Group times happen spontaneously, rather than at set times
- Staff take time to 'teach' children how to play and socialise
- The needs of all children are met within the setting – support is brought to the child

More and more young children are being diagnosed with 'conditions', the symptoms of which are behaviour-related. This increase has corresponded directly with the formalisation and schoolification of the early years. Many settings are trying to get children to do things which are developmentally inappropriate; behaviour issues emerge and a diagnosis is sought. A far better approach would be to change the practice, ensure it is appropriate for such young children and then see how the behaviour improves.

Trust that children want to be engaged, let them play, join them in their play and prepare to be amazed!

3 An enabling environment

An outstanding early years' setting is a complex organisation, and the environment is one piece of the jigsaw. The environment can support all children to be fully engaged in purposeful play of their own choice and interest. There are some underlying principles, and these are outlined here. However, it is the level of involvement of the children that should be your main measure of success. As you read this chapter, try to formulate a plan for the development of your environment, and then, if necessary, you can try to fundraise and/or find time to put the plan into action. If possible, involve the whole staff team in making the changes. A makeover day can be a superb team-building INSET day and, once involved in developing the environment, the staff take ownership and will be more likely to help with maintenance going forward. There is a suppliers list in Appendix J.

Individual interests

Practitioners realise that if they can tap into the current interests of each child, then this will lead to deeper engagement and learning. However, I worry that in some settings, the staff are trying to do this by providing different resources for each emerging interest. This is just not possible and also not helpful in terms of learning. For example, if you have children interested in pirates, caravans, outer space, the police, etc., you cannot possibly resource each interest. Think instead about how the resources that you choose to have in your setting can be used to meet all interests. For example, a cardboard box can be turned into a pirate ship, a caravan, a rocket or a police car! Blocks and Lego can be used in the same way. Therefore, look at the opportunities that your environment offers and the versatility of your resources and trust that the creativity of the children will lead them to find ways to explore their emerging interests. I would also stress that a 'current interest' is just whatever has caught the child's attention in that moment. This can change from moment to moment, or it can last for several minutes, or an hour or several days. Each child is different, and some have very pervasive interests or patterns of learning, while others have numerous interests in a day and do not have particularly noticeable 'patterns' or 'schemas'. The challenge is to engage each and every child in purposeful play by providing an environment and resources which can support this.

Workshop set up

I am advocating that child-initiated play should be happening for the vast majority of every session. Although this book is based on the 2–3 room in a preschool, I would advocate the same approach for all children in the early years and year one. This means that the children choose where to go and what to do from the moment they arrive – they initiate their own play, and adults join them and support them in their pursuits. I visit many settings where the practitioners say that the children can choose what to do, but the choice is limited by what the practitioners have already selected and put out. In order to support genuine choice, you need to have a **workshop** setup. This means that in all areas, the resources are available and accessible to the children at all times, but nothing is set out. The children need to be able to select any resource and use it in the way that they wish (within the agreed boundaries as described in Chapter 2). So, therefore, **the areas are clear, stocked and tidy at the start of the day:** the sand and water are free of equipment (but the resources are available next to these areas), the climbing equipment is in its usual position at the edge of the area etc. Remember – plastic will not rot in the rain, so leave plastic resources out to save time. Shopping baskets, attached with cup hooks or cable ties, make fantastic storage units – the rain runs straight through, and it washes the resources too! These can be used for storage of the following resources: sand, water, small PE equipment, gardening and digging tools etc.

Similarly, indoors, the tables and carpet areas are free of equipment, but the resources are available next to these areas, as shown in the following photo. This is how the room is arranged when the children arrive.

For example, the unit in the next photo contains various baskets, which the children can see into and then select what they need. The train track, engines and carriages are all arranged carefully, and there are other baskets containing items that the children might choose to select to combine with the train or with other resources in the room.

When an environment is organised in this way, **the children are in control of their learning**. They are able to select the area in which to play, the resources to use in that area and what to do with them. Obviously, their choices are limited by the areas and resources available, and it is therefore crucial to have appropriate areas with varied, high quality, open-ended resources. It is also vital that the areas are well stocked, tidy, clearly labelled or shadowed and arranged to allow optimum access. Each cohort of children will be different, and their interests and curiosities will change over the period of the year. Staff should constantly review and reflect on the environment to see which areas are proving productive and which need altering.

Shadowing of resources is used to aid tidying – as seen with the play dough resources in this photo. The "shadows" are cut from coloured card or paper and glued to the shelf. The whole shelf is then covered in 'sticky back' plastic to stop the 'shadows' peeling off (and to stop the children peeling them off). This shadowing will remain in place for several months, and possibly longer, – a task worth doing! The shelving seen here is a bookcase, and open shelving such as this is a valuable storage idea, a better option than draws or cupboards.

If shelving like this is used outdoors, then a tarpaulin can be attached which is pulled over the unit at night, secured in place with elasticated rope. The tarpaulin is just visible on the unit in the photo here on the left. Shelving like this can be used outdoors for musical instruments, investigation equipment, creative resources, blocks etc.

Because the children select and access resources themselves, they know where they are from and they know where to put them back when they have finished using them or at the end of the session. Thus, tidying up is far easier in settings organised in this way, compared to settings where the adults get the resources out for the children. Indeed, the children should put the resources back when they have finished using them and before they go to another area. This is possible if the storage is simple, accessible and if there is not too much 'stuff'!

Outdoors all day

Children should have access to the gardens from the moment they arrive. It is recognised that there is more talk outside, and some children can only become deeply engaged in their play when they are outside. Staff need to value the outdoor space as much as, if not more than, the indoor space. Be very careful that you are not giving the children subtle messages that outdoors is for 'playing freely' and indoors is for 'activities with an adult'. Children read situations and will interpret them very well. The younger the child, the more important are the relationships and attachments that they form with adults. If the adults indoors are sat at a table, then the children might opt to stay there in order to get the adult attention. However, if the same adult moves outdoors and takes an interest in all that is happening outside, then the children will follow and enjoy those experiences as well.

Boys, in particular, will make better progress if they have more access to outdoors – so please open the doors and let the children outside, but make sure you go with them!

Plastic strips in the doorways keep the cold air out even when the doors are wide open – a worthwhile investment. If the door to your garden is closed at the start of the day, I would ask 'Why?' There is usually a way around any issues, and I would urge settings to find ways to have the doors open immediately. Not only does the indoor space often get left untouched (and therefore tidy), but the levels of involvement will leap, meaning greater brain activity and greater progress over time.

Less is more

In many settings that I visit, there is far too much 'stuff'! When working to develop an environment, the first task is usually to order a skip and get rid of all the rubbish, as well as resources that have not been used for years. We usually end up donating dozens of sacks of items to local charity shops too, such as resources which have been duplicated (e.g. 20 sieves, 30 boats etc.), dressing up costumes, plastic castles, pirate ships, construction toys that are too difficult or too easy for the children etc. When making these decisions, ask the following questions, and if the answer is yes, then get rid of the item in question:

- Do children display low level or no involvement with this resource (for example, letters and numbers in the sand!)?
- Do I have too many of these?
- Do I have other resources which serve the same purpose but which deliver better levels of involvement? For example, many settings have many different construction toys, and this is really not necessary.
- Can this resource be made from other resources? For example, a farm, a hospital, a carpark, a zoo, can be made from the blocks or the Lego. A Batman costume can be made from fabric or from paper and tape in the creative area. However, animals, people, cars and trains are difficult to make, so these should be kept.
- Is this resource too difficult for the children to use? For example, Polydrons are very difficult for 2-year-olds but perfect for children in Year one.
- Is this resource too easy for the children to use?
- Can this resource only be used in one way? Try to ensure that most of the resources that you keep have scope for the children to be creative in their use. So, although jigsaw puzzles do have some value, you don't need too many of these. Similarly, outdoors, a fixed climbing frame has less value than equipment that can be moved and altered.
- Is this something that the children have easy access to at home? In particular, games and apps on screens are not necessary in settings – children have these at home. Try to ensure that you are giving the children experiences that they might not get at home.

'Less is more' is definitely a phrase to keep in mind: with fewer, carefully selected resources, they are well used and easy to tidy up. If the resources are versatile, the majority can be used all year – the children will use them differently every day.

Consistent and calm

Once the environment is working (i.e. most of the children are deeply engaged for most of the day), then there is no need to keep changing it. Maintain the environment and restock consumables (paint, sand, etc.), but leave things the same. However, if the levels of involvement are low, then obviously, things have to change. If you are seeing low levels of involvement, then the following questions might need to be asked and the issues addressed.

- Do the children have long periods of uninterrupted play? If not, can this be changed?
- Can the children be outdoors all day, or if not, for long periods of two hours or more?
- Are the resources open-ended (i.e. can they be used in infinite ways)? Examples include fabric, blocks, sand, water, mud, natural resources, boxes for junk modelling etc.
- Are the resources accessible to the children, or do they have to ask for resources?
- Are there too many resources – meaning that the area becomes too chaotic and too difficult to tidy?
- Are the rules and boundaries simple and consistently enforced, ensuring that all the children feel relaxed in the setting (see Chapter 2)?
- Is the area 'zoned' to create numerous playing areas? Is the space too big/too small?
- Are there elements of risk in the environment which will challenge and engage the children – such as challenging climbing equipment, real utensils, scissors etc.?
- Can the children change the environment, or is everything fixed? For example, is there a fixed climbing frame, or are there A-frames, planks, tyres etc. that the children can use?
- Are the adults as involved as the children? Are they interacting, scanning, maintaining the environment?
- Are there areas which will encourage wildlife and mini-beasts, or has every inch of grass and mud been concealed under soft-pour and artificial grass? If so, can you create an area to attract insects etc.?

In the best settings, you will notice it is calm. This is not to say the children are passive; far from it. The children are deeply engaged, and therefore the atmosphere feels calm and purposeful. Once you achieve this, then leave the environment alone. You do not need to add enhancements or change areas. Experience will soon show you that if you do enhance an area, then the children all rush to that area, and chaos ensues. Far better to wait and see if a new interest emerges and then work with the children to develop this interest at the time. For example, if a child is at the play dough table and talks about their birthday cake, then that is the perfect time to explore this interest and to suggest that the children find something to use as candles. It does **not** need to turn into a big project about parties – adding some twigs as candles is enough. Keep things simple and in line with the child's play. Adult agendas are often too 'big' for such young children. Another example might be that a child wants a 'telly' for the baby to watch. This is a perfect opportunity to introduce some blocks as the television, and this suggestion will then be remembered and possibly used independently in future. If an adult were to make a complicated TV from a box, for example, then in the 2–3 room, it is unlikely that the child could replicate this themselves, and so this would not support their independence going forward.

Displays too should be calm and simple. Many practitioners spend hours creating beautiful displays, and I would ask "Who do they benefit?" Hessian-backed boards with large photos of children playing can be beautiful and, with appropriate captions, these can be enough to satisfy any visitors. Other boards, if they are at the child's height, can be used by the children to display their creations if they wish, and photos of families are always interesting to the children. Keep outside areas calm too – the children will bring the colour and energy.

Don't do too many labels. Another task which is a huge waste of time is that of labelling everything and adding 'words' everywhere. For example, if you are asked to add words around the water tray (as I was asked to do many times), then I would ask "Why do I need words around the water tray? Who are the words for, because the children cannot read them?" The response is often something like "Oh, they are not for the children. They are for the adults, so that they remember the vocabulary to introduce to the children." What an insult to the staff! We, as professionals, must challenge such requests and explain that a literate environment is not about having words and labels everywhere. Rather it is about using literature in authentic ways so that children see the value and power of literacy. Therefore, have wonderful picture books in several areas (including some outdoors), cookery books in the home corner, baby books next to the dolls, books about bridges in the construction area, books about animals near the animals, books about birds in the garden, and so on.

Indoors and outdoors are different

An outdoor area should allow for learning in all areas of development but should not mirror the indoors. The advantages of outdoors should be exploited – we can be much noisier, messier, bigger and faster outside. Therefore, this is the ideal place to have loud music and dancing, messy mud mixtures and challenging physical apparatus. It is also the place to learn about and experience the weather – wind, rain, snow or sun – and to explore the natural world of mini-beasts, birds, pond life and plants – with a productive vegetable and fruit area being one of the most challenging but valuable possibilities. But often the most important learning that happens outdoors is the development of personal and social skills and self-regulation. In this large area, the children might have more chance to be independent and to take risks, and through this they learn to negotiate, cooperate, assess possibilities and dangers and take control of their own learning. Communication and language develop at a greater pace than indoors too, and physical development, particularly gross motor development, is clearly easier to promote outdoors in large spaces and on large equipment, trees and logs etc. The only area that I would duplicate outdoors is a reading area, somewhere cosy and protected from the wind where children can look at books. This is essential for those children who never choose to go indoors. All other aspects of learning can be covered outdoors with different equipment, but having opportunities to sit with an adult and look at a book should be available both indoors and outdoors.

The indoor area should also allow for learning in all areas of development but should not mirror the outdoors. There are many advantages indoors that should be exploited. It is dry, with a controllable temperature and no wind. Therefore, this is the ideal place for children to be calm and quiet (and staff should ensure this happens with firm and consistent reminders), pursuing activities which require small equipment and using resources that will not survive the outdoor elements.

Five minutes to set up

If you develop a workshop set-up, then indoors and outdoors should only take a few minutes to set up. Indoors, the water tray needs to be filled, snack area prepared and the creative area restocked. Your garden too should only take five minutes to set up, and then you will use it every day. If it takes too long to set up, then you might opt not to use the space on some days. There are videos available on YouTube showing various gardens being set up in fewer than five minutes. (Search Anna Ephgrave on YouTube.) The idea is that you leave out as much as possible. If items are made of plastic, some metals or natural things (logs, pine cones, etc.), just leave them out. If the resources are on shelves, then the shelves can be covered with a tarpaulin. Anything very valuable might have to be locked away (such as bikes). A few items might have to be brought out each day (such as books), but keep these to a minimum. Avoid having small items outdoors – such as small construction toys etc., as they just get lost. Equally, if your outdoor area is a 'wind tunnel', then it is going to be very difficult to have paper outside, but make sure you have other mark-making equipment such as chalks, decorators brushes to use with water, and so on.

Create zones

It is a good idea to try and break up large open spaces to create 'zones' in an attempt to stop too much 'rampaging' about (both indoors and outside). This proved particularly successful at Staple Hill when the carpet area indoors was developed to include a 'boundary'. The storage units and some dividers were set out to 'protect' the carpet area so that if a child was playing on there, then other children would not run across the space, potentially spoiling the construction that was being built. Some of the dividers are transparent (as seen behind the children in the photo here). This allows for light to come through but also allows for staff to be able to see into or out from the carpet area when they are sitting with the children.

Aim for authenticity whenever possible

Children respond to authentic resources and experiences. Therefore, keep this in mind when reflecting on your environment, the resources and the opportunities you offer. Real saucepans, for example, are easy to get hold of and appeal to young children. Equally, a real sink will entice children into an area, and their play will reveal experiences from home.

These general principles apply to all ages. Environments need to be suitable for the age of the children, with resources that are well organised and that the children can **access independently**, and with many which are **open-ended (versatile)**. An approach with a **'less is more'** attitude, and with **authenticity** in mind, will make practitioners be more selective about their resources. Babies need some different things to children in Year One, and staff working with these age groups will know what is appropriate in their rooms. However, I stress again that it is the levels of involvement that should be your measure of success. If the children are showing high levels of involvement, then the environment is working – so leave it alone! If there is low level involvement, then try to figure out why.

Maths is everywhere

In the remainder of this chapter, I will look at some specific areas indoors and outside. However, you will see that there is no maths area mentioned. This is because I prefer to think of maths as everywhere – just as personal and social development happens everywhere, so does communication and language, so does maths and so, indeed, do all areas of development.

Young children do not see maths (or any other subject) as distinct or separate from the everyday business of their play, their exploration of the world. It is just another aspect to their play and occurs in every area of a setting. The grid that follows gives some examples and demonstrates how absurd it is to try and keep maths to just one area of a class or garden. I would also recommend having sets of Numicon shapes in all areas – in the play dough, the sand, the water, the mud kitchen, the role play area, small construction area and so on.

Area	Mathematical opportunities
Outdoor PE equipment area (chalk board attached to wall nearby)	Different size balls. Keeping count or score and comparing. Comparing/measuring distances jumped or distances travelled by a ball etc. Ordinal numbers. Positional language.
Large and small-scale construction – including beads, cars, Lego, animals etc.	Measurements of structures built. Shape, size and number of blocks (or other construction toy) used. Properties of various shapes. Positional language. Sorting and classifying cars, animals, etc. Creating patterns – symmetrical and repeating, sorting and ordering by size, colour, shape with beads, cars etc.
Mud kitchen Water areas Sand areas Play dough Cooking	Capacity and associated language. Counting when creating/following recipes. Comparing size and shape of containers and cutters. Creating patterns with stones, leaves, sticks, shells, candles etc. Catching and counting fish etc. Using balance and associated language. Matching shapes to shadows on shelves to tidy up.

Area	Mathematical opportunities
Digging area	Counting legs on insects. Comparing length and thickness of worms. Language of size when digging holes.
Wheeled toys	Numicon and numeral attached for matching and numeral recognition in associated parking bays. Use of timer for turn taking. Discussion and comparison of speed. Counting and comparison of wheels.
Music area	Bells ordered and numbered. Operating CD player – selecting numbered tracks. Counting beats on drum etc. Creating patterns with sound.
Den building	Size, shape, height discussions. Counting pegs used/ needed. Discussion about capacity of den built.
Woodwork	Size, shape and related properties of various pieces of wood. Counting numbers of wheels, strings, windows etc. needed for train, bike, guitar etc. Understanding of weight of various pieces of wood and tools. Use of positional language.
Role play	Use of clocks, telephones, cookers, remote controls, money, balance, scales, recipe books, sets of plates and cutlery etc., leading to discussion, experience and understanding of concepts associated with shape, space, measure and number.
Creative area	Shapes, size, number in creations – with boxes, collage etc. Creating patterns. Sewing – size, shape of fabric and thread.
Self-register and visual timetable	Counting and comparing numbers of children. Developing language and concepts of time and ordering of events.
Books, puzzles, games	Available in carpet areas and outdoor investigation and reading area and include topics such as shape, number, colour, time, size etc.
Snack area	Shape, size of fruit. Capacity concepts with drinks. Fractions – half, quarter, etc.

A word of warning – be very careful in the use of questions when interacting with young children. It is easy to spoil a meaningful experience with an inappropriate (often mathematical) question. For example, if a child is enacting a magical tale with a monster and a princess, then don't ask how many legs are on the monster! It is not important within the play at that moment. There are far more authentic ways to introduce numbers and counting, such as when adding candles to a birthday cake or when making a model of a car and so on. Avoid hijacking play to squeeze in your agenda.

Outdoor areas

In this section, I will list some of the possible areas that you can have in an outdoor area. I have listed them in the order in which I value them (in terms of the levels of involvement that they deliver). Obviously, the age of the children in your setting will determine which sections are relevant and which are not. Readers – please trust your own judgement with regard to what will be suitable for the children in your care and remember that this book is predominantly based on the 2–3 age.

It is a good idea to have a stock of **appropriate clothing and boots** for children (and adults!) to wear outdoors. Each setting needs to decide about the rules, for example, "Do the children have to wear boots in the mud?" "Do they have to wear a coat in the rain?" Whatever the rules, just ensure that the adults are consistent and that the children are clear about the expectations. Have chairs or crates or logs available for children to sit on when changing their shoes, and, if possible, provide fully waterproof clothing so that the weather will never prevent children from going outside. Remember the phrase "No such as thing as unsuitable weather – just unsuitable clothing."

Bits and pieces

This can mean many things, but basically if you can acquire lots of items for the children to use outdoors, then, with adult support initially, they will soon become creative and engaged in constructing infinite things – dens, drum kits, boats, motorbikes, aeroplanes, swimming pools – the possibilities are endless. Many useful items can be found, but others might need to be bought. Large blocks are very expensive, but they deliver high levels of involvement and learning. They can be combined with numerous found and real resources, such as fabric, tyres, car parts, logs, ropes, crates, sticks, pegs, trays, pipes, carpet pieces etc. Start looking in skips and on building sites to see what treasures you can find. I have found several car bumpers at the side of the road, as well as hub caps and number plates. Old cable drums make great tables, bread trays combined with go-kart tyres make superb little vehicles. Children will use almost anything, and often in ways that adults would not anticipate.

Many of these resources can be left out in the open, at the edge of the area where they are to be used – logs, tyres, cable drums, pipes etc. However, some things must be protected from the rain (and should not be used on rainy days). The large blocks are one such item – very expensive and easily ruined if they get wet (unless you have bought blocks which are specifically designed for all weather use). These can be stored in a simple shed (or on shelving with a tarpaulin attached), and then this can just be closed if it starts to rain. Other items, such as fabric, can be stored in salt bins – again easy to close if the weather changes.

Space to run, jump and climb

Remember the rule is to walk indoors, and therefore a space to run outside is essential. Gross motor skills can be developed with the use of large cable drums, logs, planks, crates etc. Also, equipment such as A-frames, with ladders, a single pole, PE tables, steps etc. is useful. These can provide enough options and challenges for gross motor development. If a rope swing or a trapeze swing can be added to a tree as well, then even better! If you have two trees or two posts, you can put a rope bridge with two pieces of rope – one for the hands and one for the feet.

Bikes have been mentioned, but remember to ensure that these don't dominate the whole outdoor area. Indeed, if your outdoor area is tiny, then consider not having bikes. If you do have bikes, then ensure a variety – gliders, two-wheelers and trikes – and keep them to a clearly defined area.

If you do have a large amount of money to invest, then avoid fixed climbing equipment, as the children quickly bore of the same thing every day. The only fixed equipment that I would advocate are monkey bars or ropes and rope swings or a trapeze.

Reflect on the resources that you have and consider whether you could have fewer, more versatile resources instead. For example, the staff at Staple Hill decided to dispose of the red rocker (seen in the photo on the left), and the children very quickly became creative in the creation of another rocker. This example shows why versatile resources are so much more powerful, as they demand the children to think more and to be more creative – thus increasing brain activity and learning.

Smaller equipment (bats, balls, skipping ropes, stilts, hoops, beanbags etc.) can be stored on hooks or in baskets outside, and these can support the development of finer motor control.

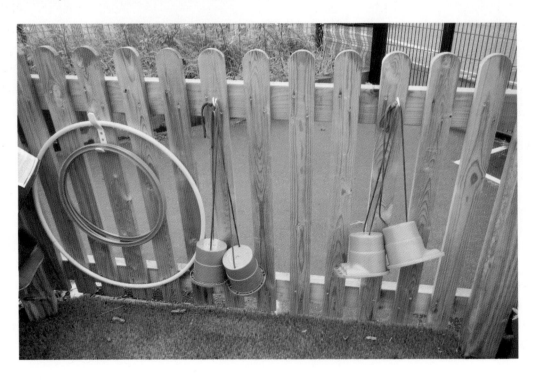

Sand

This area is one of the most popular outdoors, but the sandpit needs to be big enough for the children to get **into** the sand if possible. A huge sandpit can easily be built from logs or treated sleepers. If you opt for sleepers, these are relatively cheap to buy and can be placed directly onto a hard surface. Fixings are not essential as the sleepers are so heavy that small children cannot usually move them. Washed silver sand is ideal to fill the area, and then resources need to be stored nearby. You can attach metal shopping baskets to a fence – just hooked onto cup hooks – with a photo and word above each basket to help with tidying up. These baskets are fantastic as they can be left out all the time – the resources are plastic or natural and the rain goes through the baskets. If you have a mesh fence, the baskets can be attached with cable ties or even just placed on the ground around the sand pit. The baskets can contain buckets, spades, vehicles, moulds, sieves, natural resources (shells, conkers, twigs, stones, bark etc.). It is a good idea to have another unit nearby with plates, cutlery, saucepans etc. for the inevitable cooking that takes place, along with a small table and chairs (or a cable drum and logs) to promote role play. If possible, attach pulleys to a fence, or to any shelter above the sand and also have a large hanging balance. The sand pit can be covered with a tarpaulin at night – held in place with tyres placed on top. Another, preferable, option is netting, which deters cats and other visitors but which lets the rain through.

The sand outdoors will usually be wet – either from the rain or from water transported to the area by the children. This allows for sand castles, cakes, stews, volcanoes, tunnels, rivers and mountains etc. to be built.

You will observe high levels of involvement in this area – children are fascinated by sand, its properties and its potential. I often advise practitioners to spend a day in the sand pit – observe the children carefully in their play and find out why they are so fascinated. Don't worry about children who stay in one area for long periods or who repeatedly return to an area – remember they would not stay there if they were bored. But in order to understand what is engaging them, you need to take the time to observe their play.

Water

Shopping baskets again are ideal for storage of water resources. As explained previously, there is no need to set up the water area – the resources are left in place, ready to be used. Resources could include buckets, jugs, funnels, pipes, brushes, sponges, bottles, boats, water animals etc. A Creative Cascade Set with stands and guttering can be used to create water channels. Children will inevitably transport the water to feed the plants, wet the sand, mix with mud, pour down the pipes, fill saucepans – and many other things. A water butt is a great way to give the children access to water independently – even if you have to fill it every day with a hose.

Investigation opportunities

In many settings that I visit I find an unopened box of magnifying glasses in the cupboard. They are not doing much good in a cupboard. Bring them outside and let the children use them. It is easy to set up some outdoor shelving with bug boxes, magnifying glasses, spades, magnets etc. so that the children can explore and study their immediate environment; the weather, materials, sounds, passing vehicles, aeroplanes, mini-beasts, birds, plants and other things that they find. Try to find a space that will encourage living creatures into your garden. The smallest area of earth, with some logs or pieces of carpet, will deliver some exciting discoveries. If you can introduce other animals to your setting, this is one of the richest learning experiences for young children. Chickens (possibly even hatched from eggs), guinea pigs, rabbits and fish are all quite easy to keep, and advice is available from many organisations. Add a box of information books nearby so that these can be referred to if the children find a creature or ask a question.

Obviously, the weather is a free resource outdoors, so celebrate this and use it. The children will be excited by the wind and will be engaged, running around with ribbons and fabric or making kites. Puddles from the rain deliver endless possibilities, and shelters to get out of the rain are always challenging and fun to build. Snow and ice are magical, and in the heat of the sun, a paddling pool made from tarpaulin will keep a large group busy for hours.

If you have space for even the smallest **growing area**, then this too has huge potential for engagement and learning. By involving the children at every stage of the process, the work can be shared, and the results are then even more exciting.

Mud and mixtures

If you have space, then you can have sand, water *and* mud for the children to explore. Domestic role play will emerge in all these areas, so it is a good idea to have the pots, pans, plates and utensils to support this. Also, have some good gardening tools so that the children can successfully dig, and, again, ensure there is a water supply nearby. I would advise having the mud contained in something rather than just mud from the ground. Otherwise, there is a tendency for the mud area to expand, and the whole garden can turn into a quagmire. At Staple Hill, the outdoor area is not very large, and so they have opted to have sand and water but do not have space for a mud kitchen. The mud that is in the garden is for plants and mini-beasts.

Music and dancing

The other area that is far better suited to the outdoors is the music and dancing. A simple stage can be constructed from two pallets, with decking strips screwed down to cover the top. Simpler still is some ready-made decking pieces. Once placed near a wall, with a shower curtain as a backdrop, the stage is set. Instruments on shelving nearby along with fabric to make costumes encourage wonderful shows. Children will, however, be creative in using all sorts of resources for rhythm making and performing.

Creative/mark-making/writing

It is possible to have creative and mark-making resources outside, and this is a lot easier if your garden is protected from the wind and if you have a shelter. However, if your garden is a wind tunnel without a shelter, then you might decide that it is too difficult to store paper outdoors. If this is the case, then try to ensure that there are alternative creative opportunities outdoors – such as decorators brushes to use with water, chalks to use on the floor or a blackboard, etc. Also, you can always have paper on clipboards and mark-making equipment in tool belts or rucksacks for the children to carry around. At Staple Hill, a small shed has been stocked with appropriate resources, and this can easily be closed if the weather becomes too wet or windy. There is also a chalk board attached to the fence, and containers of chalk can be quickly put out by the children from the shed nearby.

Reading area

As mentioned earlier, the only area that I would replicate outdoors would be a book area – somewhere cosy and comfortable that children can look at fiction or non-fiction books – either with an adult or with their friends.

Role play

Children will engage in role play everywhere, but if a new interest emerges, then it can be beneficial to set up a particular role play area outdoors. This can often complement the 'home corner' that, I believe, should be constantly available (and might be indoors or outside or both). Therefore, if a child starts talking about the doctor, the café, the vets, the car wash or the police station, then this can be developed outside, using the open-ended resources described earlier. Signs and other special resources can then be made or gathered up, involving the children at every stage. Once interest in the area declines, then it is easily dismantled or changed. With children who are just 24 months old, the interest might well just last a few minutes. The interest in babies, the doctor's office, cars and cooking are more pervasive – reflecting the experiences that are familiar to children at this stage in their life. A few doctor's sets will be used continuously at this age, as will dolls, cars, cooking utensils etc. Some of these, such as the doctor's set, would be more easily stored and used indoors, whereas role play around cars, cooking, firefighting and so on can easily be facilitated outdoors. Doll's buggies are one resource which it is easier to have outdoors, where there is often more space than indoors. Again, a staff team must agree on the rules and then stick to them. I have always had the rule that indoor resources stay indoors and outdoor resources stay outdoors. This is not what would happen in utopia, but with limited budgets, it is the best option.

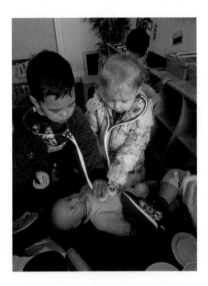

Woodwork

At the beginning of the year at Staple Hill, there was no woodwork area in the 2–3 garden, but after a few months, the staff felt confident enough to introduce this area into this garden (there is already a woodwork area in the garden for the 3- to 4-year-olds). The details about this area can be seen in the "April" section, Chapter 13.

Tiny outdoor areas

Ask yourself "What can I NOT have indoors?" and use the answer to guide you. If your outdoor area is very small, then try to include the following, (always bearing in mind that whatever is on offer indoors will be used in combination with your outdoor area):

- Bits and pieces (blocks, fabric, crates, tyres, pipes, rope, planks, boxes, etc.)
- Musical instruments
- Sand
- Water
- Equipment to develop gross motor skills (A-frames, bats and balls, skipping ropes etc.)
- Equipment to investigate the world around us

An enabling indoor environment

As with outdoors, staff should review and reflect on the environment to see which areas are proving productive and which need altering. Remember the principles – accessible, versatile resources; less is more; aim for authenticity. The **layout** of the indoors can be challenging, and staff need to reflect on which areas are causing a lot of stress, why this is the case and what can be done to reduce this. There is often too much furniture indoors, in particular **too many tables** and chairs, and the simple solution to this is to get rid of the ones that are not essential. If rooms are used for meal times, then try to source tables with removable or collapsible legs so that you don't have to have the tables in the room all day. You could also consider moving to 'rolling lunch', as happened towards the end of the year in the toddler room at Staple Hill. More information about this can be found in the June section, Chapter 15. Carpet flooring is also a big cause of stress – **wood, laminate or lino** is preferable, as it allows you to arrange the room in any way you like rather than being restricted by the location of the flooring areas that can be mopped easily. Think carefully about the location of different resources. For example, although it is essential to have opportunities for mixing sand and water outside, you might want the indoor sand to be dry to offer different opportunities. Therefore, it is necessary to keep the water tray and equipment away from the sand tray.

Staff might want to avoid making new play dough every day – so this also needs to be placed away from the water and sand. Once you identify stressful areas in the room, start asking questions. Is the construction area too small and over-crowded? If so, can it be moved or expanded? Are the children tripping over the chairs? If so, do you need to have the chairs? Children are often happy standing at tables or kneeling on the floor. Do children keep knocking down other children's models as they walk past? If so, can the construction area be protected with units in some way? Do children keep leaving rubbish on the creative table? If so, is there a bin nearby? These seem like obvious questions and obvious solutions, but it is amazing how practitioners just learn to live with such aggravations without trying to find solutions.

As with outdoors, I will look at some possible indoor areas that can be developed. Again, please think carefully about the stage of development of your children. You know them best, and you know what will be appropriate, challenging and interesting to them.

Play dough

It never ceases to amaze me how children will be deeply involved when playing with the play dough every day. The photo here shows the shelving unit containing play dough and associated resources. It is worth spending the time to create such a unit, as it will be in permanent use. Look carefully at the photo to see the variety of resources, but also note the "less is more" approach. Two pairs of scissors, rather than 20. A few cutters, not hundreds etc. There is a recipe for play dough available in Appendix K. Notice how not all resources are shadowed. Smaller items in low baskets or containers are easily visible and accessible to the children.

Cooking

The play at the play dough table, in the mud, the sand, the home corner is often concerned with cooking, something which children see happening at home. The obvious development of this play is to do some real cooking, and this is an activity which delivers deep levels of involvement and, therefore, learning. When children aged 2 or 3 are at home, they often help prepare meals, set the table and clear up. This sort of activity can be replicated in a setting, if there are enough staff. This can be a very simple activity, such as helping to cut their own fruit for snack or mixing the ingredients for a cake. Children in 2–3 provision might be as young as 24 months, but they might be 46 months. This age range is vast, and the developmental range could be even greater. There will be children who are capable of following simple recipes with adult guidance, and therefore, if ratios allow, it is a rich experience to offer to the children. If possible, create an area where cooking can happen within your room. Even if the actual cooker is elsewhere, the preparation can be done in the room. Many simple recipes can be developed that children as young as 3 can follow independently. Two such recipes are available in Appendices B and C.

Creative/mark-making

 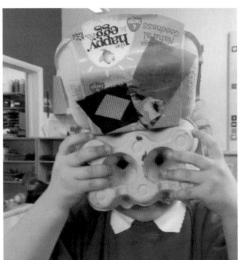

Creative development covers numerous activities from role play to painting to singing to making up stories, but here I am concentrating on the 'art' aspect of creativity: mark-making, collage, model making etc. The other thing to keep in mind with children who are in the 2–3 room is that they will enjoy being in the creative area, and they will be deeply involved doing something – but **they may well not be making anything!** It is the process that is often all-consuming at this stage of development – spreading the glue, snipping with the scissors, experimenting with the felt-tip pen, covering the paper with paint and so on. The end product is not always important – so keep this in mind when observing children at this age.

Restocking the creative areas is a time-consuming task. As with all areas, the equipment should be shadowed or labelled with a photo and word to ensure that the children can tidy up independently. Tilted storage boxes are useful for collage materials, and the Ikea kitchen rails and pots are great for pencils and pens etc. Junk modelling boxes can be displayed on shelves along with an assortment of paper and card. Other resources should include scissors, sticky tape in dispensers, staplers, hole punches, string, glue (various types), fabric and wool. Easels are useful indoors and outside along with drying racks. Many settings use ready-mixed paint, but many have developed a system which allows the children to successfully mix their own powder paints. For example, I saw nursery children dispensing powder paint stored in sugar shakers in Larkhill Nursery School in Stockport.

Literacy

As mentioned previously, young children do not segment their learning by subject. This applies to literacy as much as to any other subject. In Chapter 1, I discussed brain development in a very simplistic way. However, I do not need brain scans or scientists to confirm what experience with thousands of children has shown me – children can learn to read and write in 12 weeks when they are at an appropriate stage of development. I have seen this happen in year two on several occasions in my career. Children who join an English school in Year 2 (age 6 or 7) and who have not had formal schooling in their own country will learn to read and write in 12 weeks, often surpassing their peers who have become disengaged by seven years of the English education system. Chapter 1 also stresses how important the prime areas are. The prime areas underpin everything that is needed for a child to become literate – confidence (Personal, Social and Emotional Development), speech (Communication, Language and Literacy Development) and dexterity (Physical Development). There is a detailed section about speech and language development in Chapter 4 – stressing that much of the teaching in the early years will focus on this area of development.

As explained, the resources to support 'writing' should be in all areas, including clipboards so that the children can take paper and pens etc. to any areas they wish. I would not opt to have a 'writing area' because young children do not see writing as something separate to their normal activity – it is just another part of their play. However, the resources should always be to hand, clearly labelled, well stocked and with a wide variety of mark-making implements, paper, note books and card.

Story scribing and acting

Writing, writing, writing – every setting is worried about progress in writing. However, children can make outstanding progress in their writing – and the key is **never tell them to write!** I repeat – **never tell the children to write.** Wait for a moment when a child is interested in writing and then 'pounce'! When a child is motivated to do something, that is the moment when support and teaching will be most powerful.

One exciting thing to introduce is story scribing, which I first heard about from Vivien Gussin Paley when I was a young teacher. Whenever the staff feel it is appropriate, you can offer to scribe a story for a child. Quite often it is just a drawing that will be the initial stimulus for a story – a butterfly, a princess, a monster or a rocket. Something a child has made can be brought into a story; small world play will have a storyline, as will the role play in the outdoor areas. When writing the story, it is important for the child to watch the adult write and for the adult to write exactly what the child says. In this way, even the youngest child learns that their spoken words can be transferred onto paper. They also see how writing is formed and what it looks like. The exact words that the child says are written down, even if grammatically incorrect.

At some point during the session, the stories are shown to the group, and an adult selects some children to act as the characters in the story. Then the story is read aloud, and the children 'act' the story. When this activity is first introduced, and the children see a story being acted out, then many more of them will be keen to write a story the next day.

Mummy is walking to the park."

"go shop in car and go home and 'yummy"

Once there was a Monster in there (toddler room).
Savannah, Dolly, Holly and Lacey were hiding. 'I'm a bit Scared' said Holly.
'The monster is coming' Said Holly.
'Be quiet for the monster' Said Lacey. The monster came. He was loud. He was roaring.
Santa came and scared the monster away.

The stories are kept in the children's folders or special books and become a record of their language development, their story-writing development, their imagination, sometimes their understanding of the world (depending on the content of the story), their pencil control (if there is a picture or if they have added their 'name'). The three examples here show this clearly. They are from different children, but it is easy to see the language competence of each child at this point in time. Also note how the second 'story' was inspired by a photo from home. Stories can start from numerous initial stimuli – a painting, a photo, role play, small world play, a model, a thought, a sound and so on.

Snack area

Since we want the children to be as independent as possible and to have long periods of time to get absorbed in their pursuits, we should not dictate when they have a drink or snack. Therefore, I would recommend having a snack area where a few children can go at any time to have a drink (of water or milk) and a snack of fruit or salad items (carrots or tomatoes). This could be offered outdoors as well.

Many settings still have whole group/class snack time, and I have seen extremely low levels of involvement during such sessions as children wait for the bowl of fruit to reach them. Many practitioners worry that some children won't eat and that others will take too much. Surely this then is a teaching and learning opportunity. Once established, a snack area can be totally self-regulating, with children taking drinks and snacks that they need without overeating. If children are staying in a setting all day, then you might consider removing the snack area at a set time before lunch. When children are just 24 months old, they will need support in this area, and so an adult needs to be nearby. However, in the 2–3 room, some children will be nearly 4 by the end of their time in this room, and they are perfectly capable of being independent at the snack table. Children at this age can also be quite wasteful with fruit – taking one bite of an apple and throwing the rest away. Again, this is a teaching opportunity, but you might also want to consider offering smaller pieces of fruit and salad items to avoid waste. If the children can be involved in the preparation and cutting of the fruit, then they might be less likely to be wasteful when it comes to eating too. At Staple Hill, the parents now pay a small fee for snack each day so that all the children have access to the same snacks. Occasionally, a child opts not to have any snack, even though a parent has paid, but the staff have discussed this with parents, explained how the children are developing a life skill and that they will not be forced to eat or drink, and the parents are now fine with this. It has certainly simplified things for some parents, who no longer have to provide a snack for their child each day. There is often an adult in the snack area, and it is a perfect opportunity to sit and chat, whilst constantly 'teaching' language, social skills and physical skills.

Small world/construction/carpet area

When planning the layout of your indoor space, make sure to avoid 'dead spaces' – meaning spaces that are only rarely used, as this will mean that they are empty for the vast majority of the session. For example, at Staple Hill, one small area used to be kept empty for 'group time', but now that group time is just a couple of minutes at the end of the session, then this empty space has been put into use as the role play area. Wherever the carpet areas are, make sure they are used all the time. Clear floor space (carpeted or not) can be used for numerous activities, and the necessary resources need to be stored around the edge of the carpet. In addition, at home time (if the majority of the children leave at the same time), it helps to contain the children until their parents arrive. At Staple Hill there is just one 'exit' point from the carpet, making it easier for staff to monitor who is leaving the carpet area to go a parent.

The resources stored around the carpet could be as listed here. It is not necessary to have many different construction toys, and it is not necessary to keep changing what is on offer. Various storage units appear in photos throughout the book, but open shelving is very useful for larger items, and clear boxes, or boxes that the children can see into, are useful for smaller items. Resources will, of course vary with the age of the children, but in the 2–3 room, this list works well.

- Construction toys (Duplo, small Lego, community blocks – small and mini sets)
- Wooden train set
- Cars and other vehicles
- People
- Numicon
- Books – reference and fiction

- Animals – dinosaurs, wild animals, farm animals, sea animals, etc.
- Natural resources – stones, pine cones, sticks, shells etc.
- Variety of fabric pieces
- A few puzzles, games, threading toys, stacking toys etc. (as appropriate to the age of children)

Clearly, this list invites an infinite variety of activities. However, review the area and add or remove resources if levels of involvement drop. Staff should also insist that children tidy away the resources that they have been using before they leave the carpet. In this way it remains inviting for others. With very young children, this will be a shared venture, and often, with a child aged 2–3, the adult will, for example, put away three blocks and the child will do one. However, they are still getting the message that 'when we have finished playing with something, we put it away'.

Book area

A lovely book area is essential and should be made as inviting as possible. If there is enough space, then have a sofa, cushions, puppets and props to make the experience engaging. You can also have books in numerous areas of the indoor classroom – craft books in the creative area, cookery books in the role play, books for babies in the home corner, construction and reference books in the small world area. This is how to create a literate environment. If the children have a folder or special book, these could be stored in low units so that the children can take them out and look at them whenever they wish. In the photo here, you can see the shelving unit at Staple Hill. The staff have chosen a few books, with one book stored in each 'cubby hole'. There are some props to go with the books too – but, as seen in this photo, they have been transported at this time, but will be brought back eventually. It is preferable to a have a few carefully selected books the children can access easily rather than dozens of books squashed into a box.

At Staple Hill, the staff have included one area of books within the home corner, along with a sofa (this can be seen in the photo that follows). This has proved very successful and feels quite 'authentic'. At home, you would have books in your living room and would sit on a sofa to read to a toddler. Thus, in the preschool, I often find an adult reading to a child on the sofa or a child reading to a 'baby'.

Dry sand

Sand indoors is almost as popular as outdoors, but is usually contained in a much smaller unit. I often suggest keeping this sand dry, with fewer resources available than outdoors. On the storage unit here there is shadowing on the shelves so that the children can replace the resources independently. Not everything is shadowed, and smaller items can be placed in baskets; so could natural resources – shells, stones, twigs etc. – and cups, plates and cutlery. A 'less is more' approach has been used here as well, with a varied selection of items to ensure the sand is used purposefully. It is also worth considering resources made of metal or china to add a new dimension to the play. It is easier to have these items indoors rather than outdoors, where they might go rusty or get broken more easily. Have dustpans and brushes nearby so that the children can tidy the area independently.

Water

Water fascinates young children, and it is a vital component of any early years setting. Indoors, the water play is limited by the need to avoid flooding the whole room! The water tray should be filled every day, but the resources can be left on the shelf nearby for the children to select independently. Here is a photo of a shelving unit with water resources. Useful resources include a few boats, various containers, scoops, a water wheel etc. As with the indoor sand area, I would also recommend having some trays, the contents of which can be changed if levels of involvement drop. As a starting point for these, I would suggest shells, twigs, stones, sponges, syringes, pipettes, plastic sea and fresh water creatures. The higher shelves can be shadowed and, so long as the play is purposeful, these items do not need to be changed. Tidying up onto 'shadows' is also a game in itself. As with the dry sand, china and metal resources could be included for use in the indoor water area. Ensure that aprons are stored nearby and easily accessible for the children to support their independence.

Role play

If you ask children in key stage 2 or even key stage 3 what it is they remember about their preschool, nursery or reception, many of them will say "the home corner!" They have strong and fond memories of the 'miniature' house and the serious play that went on there. It is a vital component of young children's play as they take on the roles of the adults that they see around them. They put themselves into the position of someone else, imagine what that person would say, feel and do, and then act accordingly. This is a powerful way **to develop empathy**, which is defined as 'identification with and understanding of another's situation, feelings, and motives'. It is tempting for adults to create complex role play areas, but the home corner is the most familiar and therefore most relevant to young children. Other interests will arise during the year, and so it is a good idea to have another area – either indoors or outside – that can be used to create a 'pop-up' doctor's, vet's, shop etc. But the house should be kept permanently – both indoors and outside if possible. As with all areas, try to organise the area so that the children can tidy it easily. Therefore, particularly indoors, limit the amount of resources. So you should have three or four dolls (not 23 or 24!) and just four cups etc.

Again, use the levels of involvement to determine whether you have got the provision right – too many resources and the children can't organise them to play purposefully, too few resources and the children might not have enough to do. In either case the levels of involvement will be low. When the resources are appropriate – in the amount, variety and complexity – then involvement will be high. It is possible to have real or very realistic resources, but children will use anything to maintain the play, so a piece of Numicon will become a biscuit, a wooden block will be a mobile phone and a cushion is a perfect doctor's examining table.

ICT

ICT (information and communications technology) covers a broad range of activities and equipment. I will look first at the aspect of technology that is causing practitioners the most concern – screens – on PCs, tablets, phones, game consoles etc. As I have stated, we use levels of involvement to assess whether an activity is engaging and valuable for the children. A child can appear to be deeply involved when operating a game on a screen. However, a child on an iPad is often silent, solitary and immobile – that means that they are not developing their speech, social skills or physical skills during that period – these are the critical 'prime areas', and this alone should make us question their value or appropriateness for children under 5.

When using screen technology, only a small part of the brain is 'lit up' rather than the large areas that are lit up during other activities, such as building a den or climbing over an obstacle. The addictive nature of such devices has also been proven, which will come as no surprise to many who have watched children become more and more obsessed with screen-based activities. We must then question and re-evaluate their use in our settings and promote 3D active experiences rather than 2D passive experiences.

When evaluating screens in a setting, we should also take into account the amount of time that children are spending looking at screens when at home. When computers were first introduced to settings, it was something that many children would not have access to elsewhere. However, every mobile phone is now a powerful computer, and 18-month-old babies know how to access certain apps by touching screens. With so much exposure to ICT at home, this again must make us re-evaluate its use in our settings.

One other factor is that, because of the increase in technology in the home, children are spending less time playing outdoors and playing with creative equipment (construction toys, art equipment etc.). Therefore, it is even more important that educational settings offer the experiences that children are not getting at home. We need to increase the amount of outdoor, active, creative, independent play that is not available elsewhere. Another reason to re-evaluate the use of screens. If you do have iPads, they can be used to take photos and videos and to look up information on the internet (rather like an instant encyclopaedia).

Other equipment can be used in numerous areas of a setting – indoors, you can have cameras, digital clocks, programmable toys, CD players, door release buttons and a variety of role play equipment that requires technology – microwave, TV, kettle, toaster, cash register, remote control, mobile phone, iron, calculators, digital scales etc. Outdoors cameras can still be used, as can the CD player, metal detectors, walkie-talkies, telephones and further role play equipment.

The one piece of equipment that I would suggest to remove from settings are the PCs. Staff often report problems caused by the PCs (in terms of supervision, arguments, obsessive behaviours), and I do not feel these are outweighed by the benefits. The iPads can be used in the same way, but are far easier to remove or switch off, and they are more versatile in their use. At Staple Hill, their large PC unit was sold through an auction site, and the money raised was used to buy some wooden blocks.

Summary: Any area or resource can be evaluated by assessing the levels of involvement that the children display. Children display the highest levels of involvement when they have autonomy, when they are pursuing their own interests in an environment that allows them to be creative, take risks and challenge themselves in their endeavours. The physical environment needs to be well laid out and equipped with high quality, open-ended, varied and authentic resources.

4 The role of the adult

In any setting, there are numerous roles that an adult has to undertake on a daily basis. In a provision catering to 2- to 3-year-olds, there are many practical tasks each day before the children arrive:

- Ensuring the environment is ready (the water tray is filled, the creative area is restocked, the food for snack has arrived, covers have been removed from units in the garden and so on). The environment will not change each day, and in fact, consistency is key to ensuring that the children feel confident and independent because the environment is predictable and constant.
- Registers are ready to complete as children arrive.
- Practical tasks have been assigned if necessary. In many settings, staff will have a (hopefully loose) rota for tasks that will need to be completed during the day. For example, nappy changing, snack preparation (as necessary for the age of the children), lunch supervision, lunch breaks, and so on.

Once the children do arrive, there are further practical tasks that need to be carried out:

- Welcoming the children and talking to parents/carers.
- Ensuring registers are completed.
- Ensuring all areas of the setting are supervised (preferably without the need for a rota).
- Carrying out nappy changes, restocking, dealing with accidents, dealing with spillages and so on, as well as completing any associated forms (accident/incident forms and so on).

However, the main role of the practitioner, once the children are in the setting, is **to interact with the children as they play.** The bulk of this chapter will be describing what that means in a setting where the children are initiating the play.

In this book, I have explained that **deep level involvement indicates brain activity** and progress. Deep involvement will not occur unless a child has good levels of **well-being**, and therefore this must be the priority. This means a focus on building relationships and meticulous planning of transitions and induction. Once a child is 'settled', feels secure and trusts the adults, then their innate desire to learn can emerge. The best levels of involvement are then seen when children are allowed to initiate their own play. Therefore, I recommend arranging your settings to **maximise the amount of child-initiated play** (including access to outdoors) – if possible for the whole session. Where interruptions are essential, then make sure these are at the beginning or end of a session and make sure they are appropriate for the developmental stage of the children. **Clear boundaries and expectations are essential** so that children understand that the adults are in charge and they can relax and 'be the children' within the given boundaries. Another essential element to high-quality child-initiated play is an **enabling environment**, and Chapter 3 dealt in detail with how this can be delivered to maximise engagement. Once we trust that children are hard-wired to learn, we have ensured their well-being, rules are clear and consistently applied, children have long periods of time to play and there is a superb environment, then the levels of involvement will leap. Children will become engaged and purposeful in their play – demonstrating 'concentration, creativity, energy and persistence' – all the signals of Level 5 involvement. Children, whatever age, want to be in this state, they want to be engaged, they want to be learning and they don't want to be bored.

Once everything is in place, as has been described so far, you will see children who are at Level 5 involvement, meaning that they are making progress. Most of these children will not be near an adult.

This book is focused on the 2–3 provision, and the adult-child ratios are constantly changing. Each time a child turns 3, the ratios change (in line with the legal requirements in the UK at present). With the 2-year-olds, the ratios are 1 adult to 4 children. But when children turn 3, the ratio changes to 1 adult for 8 children. In all settings it is essential that we recognise that the children are learning at all times, even when they are not with an adult. Indeed, some of the most powerful learning happens when the children are figuring things out for themselves, struggling to master a new skill, cooperating in a group or consolidating previous learning by practising something over and over. Settings need to be organised as described to ensure that most children are engaged independently of the adults. This means that they are learning at all times, engaged at all times and progressing at all times. Scan your setting and check that the children are indeed deeply involved, whether with an adult or not. This is a sure sign that your setting is working.

What, then, are the adults supposed to be doing while the children are playing? To answer this question, I will describe how the best practitioner operates, and this will give readers a chance to reflect on their own practice. I would also recommend that practitioners read Julie Fisher's book *Interacting or Interfering*.

The adult goes to the children. They do not call the children to them. The children are pursuing their own interests and are deeply involved in their play. The best adult will **scan the area** and decide where they think they are most needed or could be of most benefit. In the photo that precedes this paragraph, we can see 12 children deeply involved in their play. Looking at this photo, I hope practitioners will see that if you called a child away from this area, you would actually be stopping this engagement, you would be stopping the learning. It is critical, therefore, that the adult goes to where the children are engaged and interested because they are already invested in the play, challenging themselves, interested and keen to take the play further. Thus, there might be an opportunity for the adult to add something to the situation. In addition, by scanning, the adult will notice if any children are not engaged and can then assess the situation to decide if this is just a transition moment (when a child has finished one activity and is just about to move on to another) or if the child does indeed need support of some kind to return to deep-level involvement.

The adult goes to the child's level. It is essential to crouch down or kneel or sit so that your face is at the same height as that of the child. Early years' practitioners have an exhausting job – getting up and down from the floor all day is just another thing that they do constantly.

The adult is interested, open, relaxed and smiling. The most vulnerable children are expert at reading the body language of adults. They may have had to learn to do so at home in order to stay safe. However, all children will learn which adults they can trust and which are a 'bit moody' or which ones shout a lot and which are not really interested in their play. It is interesting to watch a setting and to note which adults are accepted into the play more than others. Children are quite astute at 'reading' adults and will engage with those that they can trust and who are genuinely interested in the children.

The adult listens, watches and waits . . . and waits . . . and waits. This is probably the piece of advice I give to practitioners more than any other. "Just be quiet and **wait.**" Waiting seems to be very difficult for a lot of practitioners, but it is the key when working with the youngest children.

While the adult is waiting, they are PLANNING how, or if, to respond. The best practitioner will be observing the children and thinking about what they see and hear. This means they are assessing. From this they will decide how to proceed – this is planning. At this point, they might decide that the group or the child is deeply involved in their play, making superb progress, and that they, the adult, cannot actually add anything useful to this particular situation. At this point then:

The adult might decide to move away. It is very easy to spoil a child's play, and sometimes it is better to leave them and move away. There will always be other children who will benefit from the adult attention.

Once the adult finds a child or a group which they do want to interact with:

The adult will let the child initiate the interaction. If the child initiates the interaction, then the adult can be assured that it is the child's agenda, the subject is something they are interested in and something that they are invested in. Quite often **the child will ask a question.** This is so much better than situations (which I see all too often) in which the adults are constantly asking questions. **The best practitioner will be *answering questions* rather than asking them.** In the photo here, Kaz has already been observing Betsy for a while and has noticed that she is struggling to cut a piece of string.

Betsy has asked for help, and so Kaz facilitates the process by holding the string taught. She then observes that Betsy is holding the scissors awkwardly and then makes another decision about how to respond.

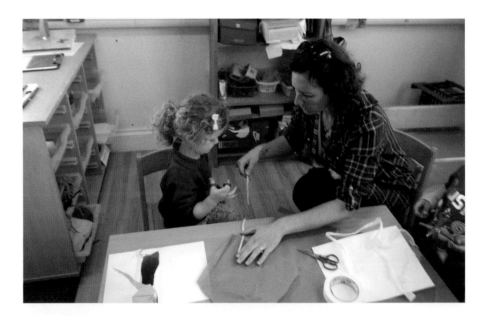

The adult will then respond as appropriate. Adults who work with young children know them 'inside out' as unique individuals. The adults are therefore able to tailor their response to the particular child, in the particular situation, at that particular moment. They can spot the unique '**teachable moment'.** This is the ultimate in differentiation. Kaz knows Betsy very well. She knows that she is confident enough to take a little bit of direction without feeling overwhelmed by this. Therefore, Kaz decides to correct Betsy's hold of the scissors so that she can use them more effectively. With another child, for example, if it was the very first time that a child had interacted with her, Kaz might not have corrected the grip in that moment. Such decisions are being made hundreds of times each day by each practitioner. Their skill has developed over time and is honed with their increasing knowledge and understanding of each child.

The adult will respond in a way that will help the child to make progress.
In other words, the adult will teach. There are many things that a practitioner can do in order to help a child to learn. They could be

> "communicating and modelling language, showing, explaining, demonstrating, exploring ideas, encouraging, questioning, recalling, providing a narrative for what they are doing, facilitating and setting challenges."

This quote comes from the current Office for Standards in Education (Ofsted) inspection handbook and can be very useful in supporting practitioners to think carefully about how they respond to children in their setting. This is actually part of the Ofsted definition of **teaching in the early years.**

In the previous example, Kaz explained and demonstrated how to hold the scissors and then encouraged Betsy to try, facilitating this by positioning her hand onto the scissors appropriately. She also provided a narrative throughout the process: "That's right, turn the scissors this way, put your thumb here and your finger here. Now open and shut, open and shut."

The adult will ponder if they want to find out something. By saying "**I wonder** how . . ." or "**I wonder** why . . .", a practitioner is saying to the child "I don't know the answer to this, but I am really interested and I am thinking about it." This allows the child time to respond if they wish, it tells the child that the adult is genuinely interested and that the adult doesn't know everything, and it encourages the child to think. It is far better than asking "What are you doing?" or "What shape is that?" Closed questions such as this do not add anything to the situation, rather the adult is just 'testing' what the child already knows. I often quote Julie Fisher when talking to practitioners, and Julie would say "Don't ask a question if you know the answer." Such a simple yet powerful piece of advice.

The adult will reflect on the impact they have had. If the adult has responded in an appropriate way, then the child will have remained engaged and will have made a step of progress (sometimes a very tiny step). Practitioners will know if their interaction is inappropriate if the child loses interest but also if the situation has not changed as a result of their involvement. In the best settings, the adults are constantly interacting with the children and moving their learning on in tiny steps, without disrupting the powerful vehicle which is their child-initiated play. To support this reflection, it is helpful for staff to consider "What would have happened if I hadn't been here?" This helps them to realise how much impact they are having. Over time, the progress of the cohort of children in such settings is outstanding. This is because as many 'teachable moments' as possible are spotted and exploited by the staff.

The adult is constantly observing, waiting and responding. They are not writing. In many settings that I visit, the adults are often writing on Post-its or clipboards or typing notes into a tablet. Writing up observations, whether onto paper or electronically, does not impact on the children. It is interacting with (i.e. teaching) children that will have an impact. Although there is a need to have evidence of what a child can do, the vast majority of this evidence will be in a practitioner's head and does not have to be documented, either on paper or electronically. Most settings do keep a certain amount of evidence in a child's 'special book' or 'profile' or 'learning journey' – such documents have numerous names, but there is a tendency for the recording of this evidence to take over as the main role of a practitioner. This is a mistake. Practitioners need to be observing and immediately interacting with the children in their setting – not just writing down what they see happening. On a very practical note, it is very difficult to interact effectively, if you are holding an iPad or a clipboard, when you are outdoors, in the mud, water or sand or when supporting children in physical activities. You need both hands free and you do not need to be worrying about the iPad getting broken, wet or dirty. If you need convincing about this, then try one day when you do not take anything with you as you go and join the children in their play. At the end of the day, reflect on how the day felt, how it affected the quality of the interactions and also the things that you remember from the day.

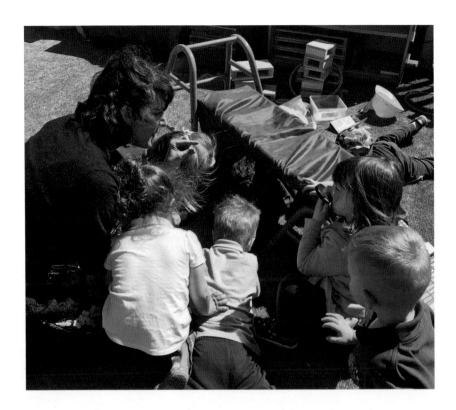

The adult will focus on the prime areas for the younger children. If you are working with children in the early years, then the prime areas and the characteristics of effective learning must take priority. In particular, as explained in Chapter 1, many children are missing out on vital interactions in the home, and therefore we are seeing more language delay, poor social skills and delays in physical development. I want to look briefly at each of these prime areas in turn.

Personal, social and emotional development

This aspect of child development is touched upon throughout this book. It is constantly relevant to the work of anyone who spends time with children of this age. It is a stressful and, in many ways, unnatural state for such young children to be spending long periods of time with so many other children of the same age. At home, there might be older or younger siblings, but there would never be 15 or 20 other children to have to 'share with', 'play with' or 'socialise with'. Adults in settings therefore have to work extremely hard to ensure that the well-being of each child is protected whilst also ensuring that they begin to socialise and empathise with their peers in developmentally appropriate ways. Many interactions between adults and children will be concerned with this aspect of development. I would stress here that adults should accept the time spent on this aspect of their work rather than becoming frustrated or stressed by it. It is easy to think, "I need to get this sorted so that we can get back to the learning". However, it is far better and less stressful to think "Ah – this is a good opportunity to teach this child how to negotiate/empathise/be patient/take turns" and so on. So the moment is valued as a learning opportunity rather than rushed through as an annoyance or a disruption to the learning. The interaction is the teaching and learning opportunity. Don't rush to complete it in the misplaced belief that what will come afterwards is more important. The photo preceding this paragraph shows what can be achieved after several months of such interactions. It shows several very young children playing together in quite a small space and each of them has good well-being and involvement. Each child is able to be happy and engaged while involved in a child-initiated group activity. This is quite remarkable for this age group and yet it is a regular occurrence in this provision after months of developing the social and emotional skills of the children.

The simple event described here is a superb example of the type of interaction that has been occurring all year and which has led to this sort of event becoming a possibility:

> Asude puts down a pair of scissors and Betsy picks them up. Asude immediately makes a whining sound and moves her hand to take the scissors back. The adult nearby reassures Asude, saying "It's ok. Betsy can have a turn." Asude then watches as Betsy uses the scissors, and when she has finished, Asude picks them up again. Betsy and Asude smile.

This might seem like a trivial moment, but it has taken the staff months to get to this point with Asude. Early in the year, with no speech and no experience of playing with children of her own age, Asude found such situations very challenging. With dozens of interactions of this nature, she has learnt that she can allow other children to be near and to use things that she wants. She does not necessarily 'like' this 'sharing' (not many 2-year-olds do), but she has learnt that she can get through these moments without tears, anger or aggression. Imagine what would have happened if she had not learnt this life skill? Hundreds of interactions like this are happening in the 2–3 room at Staple Hill every day. Staff relish them and understand their value. They have seen the impact on the children. Months and months of this teaching has meant that the behavior in the room is now exemplary. It is actually quite astonishing to see such young children managing their emotions and remaining happy in a large group of children. The interactions of the staff are responsible for this.

A few useful phrases that the staff use are as follows:

- "*I know you are angry but I'm not going to let you . . . hit/bite/scratch. . . ."* Children at this age find it very difficult to manage their own emotions. It is important to try and step in before another child gets hurt, hold the child who is emotional and use this phrase 'I am not going to let you. . . .' Once they are calm, you can talk through the event.
- "*You look sad/angry/worried/scared etc. Mummy will be back soon/You wanted to keep the blue train/That noise is very loud isn't it? Etc. Let's look at a book for a while/Let's watch and you can have a turn soon/That noise is the hand dryer – it's ok."* (Naming a child's emotion, acknowledging it and talking them through it is very powerful. You can then talk about it later too, when they have calmed down.)
- "***When** you have put that away, **then** you can. . . ."* (There is no need to be angry. Calm, consistent and firm reminders are far more effective.)
- "*Look at xxxx. She is very sad/angry/scared."* (The important thing here is for the child to notice and 'feel' the emotions of the other child. This is the development of empathy that will ensure they will gradually avoid

doing things which cause another child to be sad/angry/scared etc.) This is far more beneficial than getting a child to say 'sorry'!

These are just a few examples, but the main message is that adults need to try and understand the world from the view of a 2-year-old and to feel the emotions (often overwhelming) that these young children feel but which they cannot yet control or understand. The most reflective staff will keep trying different approaches with different children and adapt their interactions accordingly.

Communication and language development

More and more children are coming into settings with language delay (much of this is being blamed on the increase in screen time – both for children and parents). Combined with the decrease in the number of speech therapists, the promotion of speech and language is becoming a key part of the work of early years' practitioners. Many interactions will focus on this area of learning. Staff cannot wait for a child to receive help from speech therapy sessions. Rather, they need to become skilled in this themselves. Some simple strategies can be employed to support language development within child-initiated play sessions.

If an adult spots a teachable moment when they can **enhance language development**, there are *numerous specific strategies that can be used*:

a   **An adult reflects back** what the child has said (having waited for the child to speak first!) to ensure they have understood correctly. So for example Jemal says "bird eat" and the adult responds "The bird is eating."

b   This response from the adult also then includes **scaffolding and modelling** – adding extra words to the phrase and modelling correct sentence structure.

c   In this case, because the child is at an early stage of development in spoken English, the adult should accompany the verbal response with the use of **Makaton.** This is a signing system that should be introduced to **all** children and which particularly supports communication for children with English as an additional language, children who are shy and children with language delay, but also then allows every child to communicate with every other child in the setting.

d   The response is also **tailored to the unique child.** The adults need to know the children very well in order to ensure that their response is appropriate – giving the child the correct amount of new learning – not too much and not too little. In this case the adult knew that Jemal was sometimes using the article "the" and so reminded him of this and also introduced the verb "is" as new learning. For another child in the class, the adult response might well have been different because she would have assessed and responded according to her knowledge of *that child*.

e   Staff should **avoid too many questions** (remembering that questions can be stressful and that we want to avoid stress for the children), but they should do a lot of **pondering**. For example Kiera says "Look! The ball went on the roof," And the adult responds, "Oh, it is stuck so high up. **I wonder** how we can get it down." The response has involved reflecting back, scaffolding, modelling and pondering – all tailored to this particular child. In this way, the adult **invites but does not insist on further communication**.

f   For a child who is more reticent to speak, an adult can sometimes **commentate** as the child plays – again tailored to the particular child. For example, they might say, "Oh the car is going down the ramp." The child will be hearing the language and might use it later when the adult is not there.

g   Sometimes the interaction will involve some **direct teaching**. For example, Joey says "I want this." (*He points to the rolling pin that another child is using.*) The adult responds "This is a 'rolling pin'. Can you say that? 'Rolling pin'." Joey repeats "Rolling pin."

Physical development

Babies learn to walk – eventually – if they are given the opportunity. If they are strapped in a buggy or a car seat, then they will not learn to walk. This example is how I view all aspects of physical development. We, as adults, can certainly prevent children developing physically by depriving them of opportunities to be physical – by keeping them still. However, given the opportunities, children's physicality will develop naturally, and this will be different for each child. For example, Kayla at 28 months can hold a pencil in a tripod grip, she can put on her own clothes, she is out of nappies, she can walk up stairs with alternate feet, climb ladders and swing from a bar holding on with two hands, and she can do a forward roll. She can't yet jump, she is nervous of her "wobbly" glider bike and her running is actually very fast walking. Oscar at 28 months cannot hold a pencil and cannot get dressed by himself and he is still in nappies. He can already run very fast – including up and down stairs; he can go across three monkey bars and he zooms about on his glider bike with both feet off the ground. Both these children are fine. The 'path' of development is slightly different, but neither one of them has any 'problem'.

Given further opportunities and time, both will continue to develop in their own unique way.

If children arrive at a setting having had limited physical experiences, we do not need 'interventions'. We need to give these children experiences and encouragement to build their confidence and resilience in all areas. They will eventually tackle new physical challenges. We cannot 'accelerate' this development, but we can certainly slow it down if we put pressure on young children, or if we keep them indoors, or if we try to force them to undertake inappropriate 'tasks'. Provide an enabling environment which includes a variety of physical equipment and opportunities, develop confidence and resilience, and allow the child to do the rest.

We should not record all our interactions

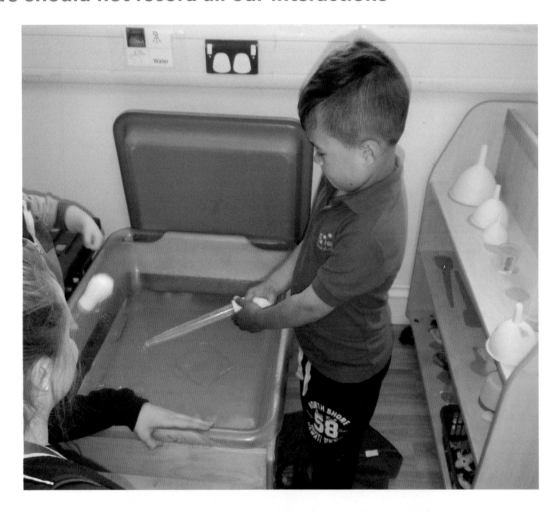

Practitioners in the early years have approximately 1,000 interactions per day. In the best settings, each of these interactions is a cycle in which the adult observes something, assesses it and responds appropriately to move the learning on – that is, they plan and teach **in a matter of moments**. This means that each day a practitioner has 1,000 interactions leading to 1,000 tiny steps of development, all adding up to result in outstanding progress over time. The practitioners are **planning in the moment** 1,000 times per day.

However, if a practitioner were to record each interaction after it has been completed, then they would not have anywhere near 1,000 interactions; they would probably have about 100 or less. Therefore, we have a choice to make. Are we going to have 1,000 interactions per day and teach 1,000 next steps, with just a small amount of documented evidence, or are we going to try and document everything that happens, thereby reducing the number of interactions to less than 100 (meaning less than 100 next steps have been taught as well)? The choice is very simple. **Let's write less and interact more.**

To summarise:

Practitioners working in a setting have numerous practical tasks which must be completed before the children arrive each day and also other tasks which must be completed during the session. These tasks include environment preparation, registers, nappies and so on. However, their most important role, once the children arrive, is to focus on relationships and well-being and to interact with the children.

The best practitioner will be constantly

● Observing the children and deciding where to place themselves
● Moving to where they decide they are needed most
● Going to the child's level
● Being interested, relaxed, smiling and maintaining open body language
● Watching, listening and deciding how, or if, to interact
● Allowing the child to initiate the interaction
● Avoiding closed questions – pondering about unknown things
● Responding in a way that will add something to the situation, rather than just 'testing' what the child already knows
● Focussing mainly on the prime areas with children aged 2–3 years
● Reflecting on the impact that they have had
● Avoiding writing while interacting

Each practitioner has approximately 1,000 interactions each day. Within each interaction they are 'observing, assessing, planning and then teaching'. Therefore, they are teaching 1,000 next steps each day as well. If we get this aspect of our work right, then the progress of the children over time will be outstanding.

5 The paperwork

Building on the previous chapters, which considered the key principles of child-initiated play, this chapter considers the supporting paperwork. However, the paperwork that accompanies the best early years' practice is the least important part of that practice. If you haven't already read the previous chapters, I urge you to read them first. An understanding of brain development will give you the confidence to explain why child-initiated play, above all else, is the best way for children to learn.

Chapter 1 explains that child-initiated play leads to deep levels of involvement – indicating brain development and progress. To organise a setting which ensures that as many children as possible are displaying this deep level of involvement is a hugely complex task.

Chapter 2 considers many aspects of practice that need to be considered if the 'play' is to be successful. Thus the chapter looks at how it is critical:

- To always prioritise and support the well-being of the children – primarily through establishing secure relationships with one or more adults.
- To have every member of a team and the parents 'on board'.
- To have appropriate routines in place, with long periods of uninterrupted 'play'.
- To establish and maintain the expectations and 'rules' (within which children can feel safe and relax).
- To ensure the provision can meet the needs of all children, including those with additional needs.

- To ensure that staff are supported and trained to feel confident in their role.
- To have manageable, effective systems of record keeping and tracking.

Chapter 3 is huge and explores the critical factor that is an enabling environment. Without a superb environment, it will be very difficult to have all children engaged and learning through child-initiated play.

Chapter 4 considers the other critical factor, which is the role of the adults. The chapter considers all the practical tasks that adults have to do in a busy setting, but focuses mainly on their role within child-initiated play – which is to observe, assess, plan and teach – **in a matter of moments** – that is, having quality interactions. This has recently become known as **planning in the moment**, but, please remember, **this is nothing new**; it is just good practice. This is explored further in Chapter 4.

In this chapter, I am going to describe the paperwork that has been developed as a way of recording some of the teaching cycles that occur thousands of times each day in a setting where children are initiating their own play. However, I stress again that this chapter alone, explaining a new format for paperwork, will not improve your practice. It is the practice that has to change first, and then you can re-examine the paperwork that supports the practice.

This book has explained why child-initiated play is so valuable, and I am advocating that this is what children should be doing for most, if not all, of their time in a setting. We are looking, in particular, at children aged 2–3 and, with this age, they should **never** be called away from their play during a session. They should not be doing focussed activities, subject specific lessons, interventions, group times or whole group snack time. They do not need to be told what, where or how to play. Within the given rules and boundaries, they should have the **freedom to learn** in a way that suits them and about the things that interest them. If children have genuine choice, then it is impossible to predict what they are going to choose to do, and therefore it is impossible (and a waste of time) to try and pre-plan what they will do. The adult's role is purely to observe the play, assess what they see, plan how (or if) to respond and then teach next steps immediately in a way that is uniquely suited to the particular child in that particular moment.

Each adult will be doing this hundreds of times each day. It is not necessary or desirable to record all such teaching cycles, and the remainder of this chapter will describe a tried and tested model for recording a sample of these cycles. The sample is sufficient to meet all legal requirements, and enough in terms of documented evidence about a child, but, more importantly, it is enough to keep parents informed and involved and enough to give the children a unique record of their time in a setting.

In the simplest terms, the children are all initiating their own play, and the adults are interacting with all the children, teaching next steps as often as possible. Each week they will select a few children to be the 'focus children', and the adults will record some of the interactions that they have with these focus children. If you have a child who has 1–1 support in your setting, then I would recommend that they are, in fact, a 'focus child' every week. This will ensure that you have a record of how the extra support for that child is being deployed and what impact it is having on the child.

Focus children and parental involvement

Each week, usually on a Friday, staff select the 'focus children' for the following week. This is 10% of the group for children aged 3 or over – so if you have 10 children in the room who have turned 3, then one of them will be a focus child each week. For the younger children – aged under 3 – staff select 20% of the group to be the focus children, as they have higher staff ratios and the children make progress more rapidly. So if there are 20 children aged 2, then four of them would be the focus children. In settings where children do varying numbers of hours and sessions, then decide for yourself what is a manageable amount. Don't start with too many, as it will take time to get used to the recording of interactions, and it is easier to just focus on a few children at a time. I would not advise choosing one child from each key person. In fact, it is better to select all the focus children from one key person, and then all staff will get to know those children. If you choose 10%, then each child will be a focus child once per term. If you choose 20% (for children aged under 3), then they will be a focus child each half-term. When there are a lot of new children, I recommend that you choose children who have settled quickly, show good levels of involvement and appear quite confident. There are many reasons for this: – they will be able to cope with some close attention; they are confident enough for staff to give them some appropriate challenges; also, their Learning Journey sheet (see details later) will be completed quite quickly – this is important at the stage of the year when staff are having to work hard with the settling of many of the other children.

Once the children have been selected, they are given a parent consultation sheet to take home (see Appendix E). The parents are also invited to share some photos from home – this could be via email or uploaded if you have an online system. Staff should speak to the parents and explain that the family should fill in the sheet in as much detail as possible and also take some photos over the weekend. Because you are only trying to get a few parents each week to complete these sheets, it is possible to approach them individually and remind them. For some parents, they might want someone to scribe their responses for them and staff will know which families this is likely to apply to. Some parents might feel more comfortable filling these electronically so they could be emailed to parents. I would recommend that you create your own sheets for your parents. Below are two examples of completed parent sheets.

Parent's Comments for Focus Week

Week beginning __Oct 8th__ we will be focusing on your child. We will be observing them while they play to find out more about their interests and how they are progressing. Please take some pictures (no more than 10) of your child enjoying activities out of pre-school. Please email them to info@staplehillstars.co.uk. We value the knowledge and understanding you have of your child and would really appreciate it if you would share this with us so that we can work towards your child's learning and development together.

Name of Child: Betsy Hathway	Date 10/10/18

Parent/ Carer Comments:
You may wish to comment on.
What do they like to do/ play with at home? The interactions/ conversations they had with others during the observation.
Is there anything significant happening in your child's life at the moment e.g. visits, new pet, family celebrations?

Betsy really enjoys looking at books + naming objects inside
She takes out her animals + lines them up on the table
She will often look at photos + talk about (possibly a schema).
Loves singing baby shark (all the time!)   family members.
If you ask her to do anything eg- nappy change etc, she will say 'Elsie' +
will use quite a few makaton signs - house, duck, bird   .point
Loves food!!   We celebrated nannys birthday at the weekend with   love
                                                          chocolate cake!! action songs

Do you have anything you would like to ask about your child's progress and development?
Are they settled ok - can be busy at drop off + pick up so feedback
at a stay + play would be great!!   + any peers
be nice to know what their interests are at pre school,   they play
                                                          with

Signed- Hathway   date- 10/10/18

Please return this sheet by __ASAP__
Please note that we do have one camera that we can loan out for a week if you are unable to take photos.
Please see your child's key worker to arrange an appointment to discuss your child and book in to stay and play with your child during a session.

The consultation sheets are returned after the weekend and the photos are uploaded or emailed into the setting. The information provided by the parents is fascinating, and staff often find out about events that the child might never have revealed – visiting relatives, family events, new pets etc. The completed sheets can be stored in the child's folder or special book or photographed and stored electronically – a lovely example of the parents' voice. The photos will often link to this information and can prompt the child to talk about these things. In my experience, many of the photos show children getting involved with cooking at home, spending time at the shops and with relatives.

You can print some of the photos from each child to put in their folder or special book and note down anything that the child says about the pictures.

Talking about his photos with a peer.

"Mcdonalds, me have burger".

(T) wonders whos in the picture with Leo?
"Leah my brother"
(T) models language "your sister"
"Yeah Leah my sister".

"Look my snow man"
(T) wonders what Leo has used for eyes + nose?
"Food" he tells me

"Look chocolate Iceream Leo says laughing

Planning in the moment for individual children is recorded on Learning Journey sheets

On Monday one Learning Journey sheet is put up on the planning board for each of the focus children (see Appendix F and G). I would advise you to create your own sheet and adapt it to suit your setting. You will see in the appendices that there are two different sheets. One can be used for any child in the 2–3 room, and one is for any child who has additional support because of an additional need. You could, however, just use a blank sheet of paper, as it is basically just somewhere to write up some of the significant interactions.

The Learning Journey sheets gradually fill up

The Learning Journey sheets are blank at the start of the week, except for the name, date and a couple of notes to remind staff about any particular areas that they wish to focus on with this child and anything that the parents have asked about. You will find several examples of completed learning journeys at the end of this chapter. Towards the end of this year at Staple Hill, the staff decided to review and amend the Learning Journey sheets. They were finding that once something was written in the top left-hand box of the sheet (areas for focus) – it was sometimes difficult for staff to interact freely. Some staff felt that once something was written in that box, then they felt obliged to try to ensure it was covered during their interactions with the child. This could result in them 'hijacking' the child's play in order to divert it onto this aspect of learning. The staff team has decided to remove this box from the learning journey, and the new style learning journey that will be used going forward can be found in Appendix H.

There is no forward planning

In the Introduction, I explained the theory behind this approach. In brief, you need to set up an enabling environment that is the best you can possibly have and then allow the children to learn by initiating their own play. The staff observe and interact with the children in their pursuits – looking out for 'teachable moments' in which they can make a difference. Some of these interactions with the focus children are then recorded on the learning journeys. All adults who interact with a focus child contribute to the learning journeys. This process contains a moment in which the adult has to 'plan' what to do as a result of what they have observed.

In many settings, observations are made, the plans are written down and the activity is delivered at a later date. With the system that I am advocating, staff do not do any such forward planning – rather they remain 'in the moment' with the child and respond immediately. If a child is concentrating on using the scissors at 2 pm on Monday, that is the moment in which a skillful adult can interact with that child and 'teach' them how to use the scissors effectively. The child is motivated and interested in that moment and therefore keen to learn. Such an interaction might appear on a learning journey as follows: 'T' indicates 'adult'. Note that the record of the interaction includes the *observation*, the *teaching* and the *outcome*.

"Mia was trying to cut a piece of dough, but was holding the scissors with two hands. 'T' modelled how to hold the scissors with thumb and finger. Mia watched carefully and then copied the technique correctly. She was able to cut the dough successfully."

Interactions are recorded afterwards and the 'teaching' is included

Highlight the 'teaching' (I usually use yellow). **It is vital that the entries on the learning journeys do contain an element of teaching.** Some observations, without any 'plan' or 'teaching', can also be recorded but not included on the learning journeys – rather they are stored separately in the child's individual folder. These are usually referred to as 'Wow!' moments. But the entries on the learning journeys are intended to be a record of some planning and teaching. Therefore, they are interactions when an adult has been involved and has had some impact on the child, **teaching a next step in that moment.** There are several examples of completed learning journeys at the end of this chapter. You will notice that some of these do not have any highlighting. This is because the staff are now confident and familiar with the system. They always include the 'teaching' and therefore do not need to highlight the 'teaching' word and sometimes do not do so. However, if the system is new to your team, then I would recommend using a coloured pen to pick out the teaching words in each interaction. This will also help staff to reflect more carefully on their interactions and to ensure that they are actually making a difference through their interactions.

Another example might read:-

> *"Fabien was pointing at the banana. 'T' modelled the word banana. Fabien repeated 'banana', and the teacher passed the plate over to him."*

I visit many settings and often see plans for focussed activities or circle times related to the teaching of sharing and turn-taking. However, it is far more powerful to do this teaching at a moment when it is relevant to the children in a real situation. For example an entry on Sienna's learning journey reads:-

> *"Sienna wanted one of the hoola hoops. 'T' modelled the phrase & Sienna repeated 'Can I have one please?' 'T' encouraged Sienna to say this to the other child. Sienna did so and the boy gave her a hoop."*

The focus for the youngest children will be almost exclusively around the prime areas of personal, social and emotional development, physical development and communication and language.

With 2-year-olds, language and socials skills are often the main subject of the teaching:-

> *"Toby is trying to take play dough from Kaan. 'T' models the phrase, 'Can I have some please?' and Toby copies saying 'un sum pease?' Kaan hands over some play dough. 'T' reminds Toby to say 'Thank you.' "Toby says 'ankoo.' "*

In this example, the practitioner has written exactly what the child said, and this becomes evidence of this child's language ability on this particular day. It is a good idea to highlight the child's words in a different colour.

For older children, the focus of the teaching might be very different, but the teaching cycle is the same. The oldest child in the 2–3 room could be 47 months, and the 'teaching' for them will be at a level appropriate to their stage of development. For example:

> *"Jamie has painted a picture of 'Mummy and the big dog'. 'T' encourages Jamie to talk about what happened and scribes the story as Jamie talks (modelling writing). Later his story is read to a small group and they act out what happens. Jamie is delighted to see his story come alive."*

Next steps are taught in the moment

In all these examples, the children made progress in a very short space of time. Whenever anyone is observing child-initiated play it is important to have a member of the staff team with them in order to point out the progress being made and the 'teaching' that enabled the progress to happen. I am often asked about 'next steps' and how these are noted/remembered. I point out that when working 'in the moment', **the next steps are carried out immediately**, and therefore we do not need to record them anywhere else. I have visited many settings where they have written down literally hundreds of 'next steps', and the staff are stressed trying to remember them all and trying to find time to teach them!

The diagram here shows the traditional teaching cycle that is recognised as best practice. The timescale for the duration of the cycle is where 'in the moment' practice differs from many settings. The whole cycle is completed hundreds of times each day (some of which are recorded), whereas in many settings the cycle is spread over a day or a week, with observations happening one day and the resulting activity happening the next day or the next week.

Planning
What next?
Experiences and opportunities, learning environment, resources, routines, practitioners' role.

Start here
Observation
Look, listen and note.
Describing

Assessment
Analysing observations and **deciding** what they tell us about children.

However, it is recognised that to respond immediately is the most powerful way to teach our youngest children. The National Strategies document "Learning, Playing and Interacting" states:

> Babies and young children . . . are experiencing and learning in the here and now, not storing up their questions until tomorrow or next week. It is in that moment of curiosity, puzzlement, effort or interest – the 'teachable moment' – that the skillful adult makes a difference. By using this cycle on a moment-by-moment basis, the adult will be always alert to individual children (observation), always thinking about what it tells us about the child's thinking (assessment), and always ready to respond by using appropriate strategies at the right moment to support children's well-being and learning (planning for the next moment).

This is exactly what I am suggesting that adults should do throughout every session in their setting.

The schedule for inspectors has a useful quote too:-

> Teaching should not be taken to imply a 'top down' or formal way of working. It is a broad term which covers the many different ways in which adults help young children learn. It includes their interactions with children during planned and child-initiated play and activities: communicating and modelling language, showing, explaining, demonstrating, exploring ideas, encouraging, questioning, recalling, providing a narrative for what they are doing, facilitating and setting challenges.

These are exactly the sorts of things which I am suggesting that staff should record on the learning journeys. This quote, from Ofsted, is included in Appendix I, and I would suggest this quote is put on the wall beside the Learning Journey sheets to support staff in completing entries on the learning journeys. They can then reflect on their role – "Did I model? Did I demonstrate something? Did I provide a resource? Did I scaffold?" etc. A good tip for staff is to ask themselves "**What would have happened if I hadn't been here?**" The impact, that the adult has had, then becomes more obvious.

Staff often take photos of the events, and these can be added to the learning journey as well. By the end of the week, the sheet is full of notes and photos – a unique record of that child's learning and development in that week. There are examples of completed sheets at the end of this chapter. Practitioners who have tried this way of working report that not only are they re-inspired and happy in their role, they have also got to know the children in far more depth and as unique individuals.

Completed learning journeys are treasured and shared

The key person should keep a colour copy of each learning journey in her planning file; the original copy should go in the child's special book or folder, and a copy should be given to the parents. Again, if you are using an online system, it is possible to complete a paper learning journey and then take a photo of this to upload to the child's online profile.

Once the Learning Journey sheet is complete, you can invite the parents of the child into your setting for a discussion about the week and all that you have learnt about the child. You can discuss any points that the parents have written on the consultation form and encourage them to add comments to the child's folder. Together you can agree on possible areas for focus in future and **give the parents some ideas of things to be doing at home** to support these areas. These suggestions – for the parents – can be noted in the bottom right-hand box on the learning journey. Again, the staff at Staple Hill have reviewed the wording on the sheet and have amended it as shown in Appendix H. These weekly meetings with parents are so much easier and meaningful than trying to meet with all parents on the same evening. You have the learning journey to talk through and you have just spent the week focussing on the child that you are discussing, so your knowledge and understanding of that child is deep and accurate.

Staff are interacting with all the children

I stress again that, although they do give the focus children a bit more attention, the staff are interacting with *all* the children, but they do not record all interactions – they only record some of their interactions with the focus children on their learning journeys. The focus child system ensures that every child does get some records created every term (or half-term for children under 3). It also ensures that **the 'invisible child' becomes visible** as the staff seek them out during their focus week, eager to find out what the child is doing and how they can support the child to develop. Without a systematic way of keeping records, it is easy to slip back to the situation where you are recording way too much again, as interesting things are happening constantly. The system also avoids the situations in which you have far more documentation for a child that is always eager and ready to show you something and demanding your attention. The focus child system means that, even though not everything is recorded, you do still have records of learning for each child each term (or half-term).

Wow moments are recorded for individual children

Within an enabling environment and with all this wonderful teaching, the children will soon start to do things independently, and when such moments are observed they might be referred to as 'Wow!' moments. Staff should write 'snapshot' observations of these moments, but they should be when the child does something independently, for the first time. For example, "Asude made a perfect sandcastle independently" (as in the photo here) or "Jordon went to the toilet on his own and remembered to wash his hands" or "Beth said 'Help me please!' in a loud clear voice." These observations might be accompanied by a photo and should be dated and annotated to explain why they are noteworthy for a particular child. In settings that are using an online system and where they are trying to work 'in the moment', the tablets are often now just used for truly 'Wow!' moments and the entries uploaded to the child's profile as evidence of attainment.

At Staple Hill, the parents are also invited to share 'Wow!' moments from home, and they are given stars on which they can write these. Two examples of these are shown here. This is another way to strengthen the partnership with parents.

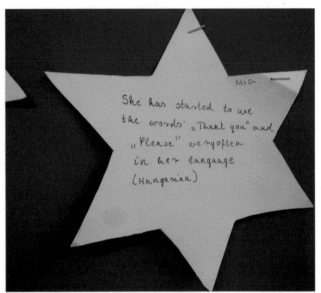

Content of folders/special books

There is no legal requirement to keep documented evidence of attainment. However, if you have read this book carefully, you will see that there will indeed be various items that will make up a child's special book or folder. This will include their stories, their Learning Journey sheets, their photos from home, the consultation sheets from parents, evidence of 'Wow!' moments and anything that the child might want to keep in their folder. However, **each special book will be unique**, because each child will have had a unique experience within the setting. The special books at Staple Hill are large stapled books, and these are available for the children to look at. Often, when I am in the preschool, I see children carefully looking through their special book and chatting about the memories it raises.

Assessment and tracking

● It is not necessary to 'cross-reference' the entries on the learning journeys to developmental milestones or any sort of tracker.

● It is not necessary to spend time cross-referencing 'Wow!' moments to any sort of tracker.

● Practitioners need to regain the confidence to recognise that the vast majority of evidence is in their heads.

● In the final part of this chapter, you can read about the way that Staple Hill have opted to track the development and progress of the children using the Early Excellence Assessment Tracker.

● In England at present, there is a legal requirement to carry out a two-year check and to assess children against the early learning goals at the end of the Reception year. There is no other legal requirement to document anything in the EYFS at this time.

● The paperwork described in this chapter is more than enough to meet all requirements – those of the Department for Education (DfE), those of Ofsted, those of the parents but, most importantly, those of the children.

Two-year check

As mentioned, at the time of writing this book, there is a legal requirement in England to carry out a developmental check on a child when they are between the age of 2 and 3. This is designed to pick up on any areas where a child's development is not 'typical' or to spot possible barriers to development. Once the report is complete, the aim is that identified areas of concern will be noted and any support that might help can be put in place. At Staple Hill, as in most settings, the owners and the staff have created their own 'format' for recording the findings from their two-year checks, called "I am 2". This can be found in Appendix D.

Early Excellence Assessment Tracker (EExAT)

The team at Staple Hill used to use a tracker that they had devised themselves, based (as is the case in many settings in England) on statements from the Development Matters document. However, staff found this overly burdensome and time-consuming, trying to track and assess hundreds of statements for each child.

They started to look for alternatives and, for the past two years, have been using the Early Excellence Assessment Tracker (known as EExAT). This is a commercially produced assessment tracker which settings can purchase from the company Early Excellence.

The system is based on the idea that we do not need to track every tiny aspect of development. Rather, we can assess children against a few 'key indicators' within each area of development. Then, if a child is meeting these indicators, they are probably developing typically in that particular area of development. When compared to Development Matters, there are approximately 75% fewer statements to consider.

In addition, the system recognises that the levels of well-being and involvement are critical in showing how well a child is learning, as well as highlighting and reviewing the characteristics of effective learning each time the tracker is updated for a particular child.

Another major difference with this tracker is that there are no 'best fit' judgements to be made. Nor do any of the assessment bands 'overlap'. The statements are listed at six-month intervals – so 6 months, 12 months, 18 months, 24 months and so on. Each statement is related to a 'typical' child at that particular age. The system recommends that practitioners assess each child when they are as close as possible to the age on the tracker. So, for example, when a child is 48 months, you should update their tracker, looking at the statements for 48 months. In this way, their development is tracked against their actual age. With each statement, the practitioner would consider the statement and ask themselves: "Can the child do this? Yes or not yet?" If they consider that the child cannot yet do the stated thing, then they would look at the statement for a child 6 months younger. The system then produces a colour-coded and visual representation from which progress is immediately visible.

For me, one of the main attractions of EExAT is that practitioners do not have particular statements in their minds when they are interacting with the children. They do not join the children in their play with a particular assessment statement in mind. The idea is that you spend quality time with the children, interacting with them, observing them and getting to know them, and then when you sit at the computer to complete the tracker, this is a simple and quick task. Staff should be able to assess a child against any of the statements by thinking about the child and considering the statement on the screen. If they are doubtful about the child's ability related to a particular statement, then it probably means that the child is not confidently or securely meeting that statement. Once staff are familiar with the software, it takes about ten minutes to update the complete tracker for one child.

The system also has exemplification materials so that staff can feel confident that the assessments they are making are in line with anyone else who is using the system.

At Staple Hill, EExAT is just used for tracking. Once all the data has been inputted, the system produces cohort tracking information and can filter data for various groups within the cohort. It is also possible to use the system to store photos and observations, and it can create reports and so on. However, at Staple Hill, they have opted to continue to use paper-based learning journeys and special books and so they have not used this aspect of EExAT.

The major benefit for the staff at Staple Hill has been that they no longer feel the 'weight' of assessment statements on their shoulders. They are free to enjoy being with the children and to allow the learning to flow in any direction. They are not restricted or diverted by trying to 'cover' certain things. They trust that the high well-being and involvement of the children is the main indicator that the children are learning, and they let the children lead. Further details about EExAT can be found at https://eexat.com.

Summary of planning in the moment

- The children are initiating their own play (for almost all their time in a setting) as this is when they are deeply involved (an indication of brain activity and progress).
- The adults do not know what the children will choose to do; therefore, they cannot plan ahead.
- The adults constantly observe, assess, plan and teach, completing this cycle hundreds of times each day.
- Each week a few children are chosen as the 'focus children' for the week. Their parents are given a consultation form, and if possible, they will provide some photos from home.
- The adults will record some 'teaching cycles' or interactions on Learning Journey sheets for the 'focus children' each week (this is 10% of children over 3 or 20% for children under 3).
- Finally, any truly 'Wow!' moments will be recorded for children when they are observed doing something independently for the first time.
- Once the learning journeys are completed for the focus children, their parents are invited into the setting for a meeting with a member of staff.

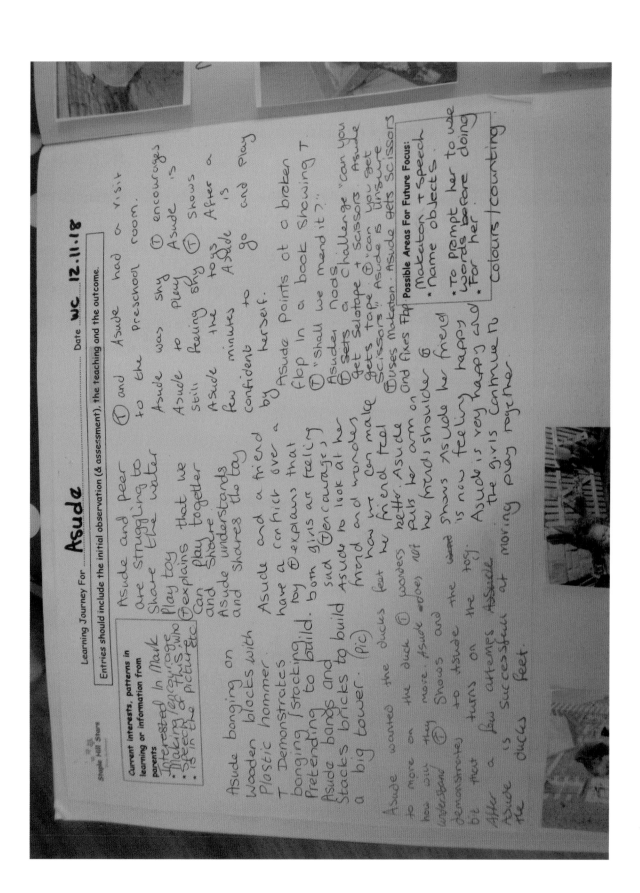

Staple Hill Stars

Learning Journey For ..Asuda..   Date ..WC.. 12.11.18

Entries should include the initial observation (& assessment), the teaching and the outcome.

Current interests, patterns in learning or information from parents

Interested in Mark Making/Language Speech of this who is in the picture etc

Asuda banging on wooden blocks with Plastic hammer. Asuda T Demonstrates banging/stacking to build. Pretending to build. Asuda bangs and Stacks bricks to build a big tower. (Pic)

Asuda wanted the ducks to move on the duck T wonders how will they more. Asuda does not understand T Shows and demonstrates to Asuda turns on the bit that turns on the toy. After a few attempts Asuda is successful at moving the ducks feet.

T and Asuda had a visit to the Preschool room.

Asuda and Peer are struggling to share the water Play toy T explains that we can Play together and share Asuda understands and shares the toy.

Asuda and a friend have a conflict over a toy T explains that both girls are feeling sad T encourages Asuda to look at her friend and wonders how her can make her friend feel better. Asuda puts her arm on her friends shoulder & shows Asuda her friend is now feeling happy Asuda is very happy and the girls continue to play together.

Asuda was shy Asuda to play still feeling shy Asuda the toys few minutes confident to by herself.

T encourages Asuda is T shows After a is go and play

Asuda points at a broken flap in a book showing T. T "shall we mend it?" Asuda nods T sets a challenge "can you get Sellotape + scissors. Asuda gets tape. T "can you get scissors". Asuda is unsure T uses Makaton. Asuda gets Scissors and fixes flap

Possible Areas For Future Focus:
* Makaton + Speech
* Name objects.

* to prompt her to use words before doing
* For her.

Colours/counting

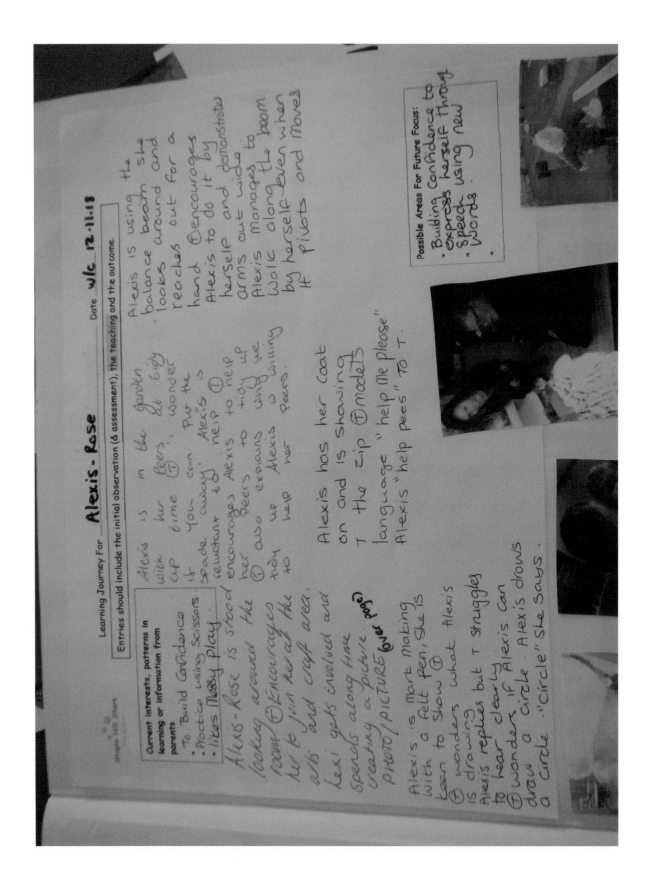

Simple Hill Stars

Learning Journey For ......**Reuben**...... Date **26.11.18**

Entries should include the initial observation (& assessment), the teaching and the outcome.

Current interests, patterns in learning or information from parents

- Imaginative play-vehicles, fire, home corner
- Singing and props
- Father Christmas

Reuben joins (T) in the garden, the wind is blowing. (T) encourages Reuben to listen and look at the effects of the wind. (T) selects a piece of fabric and it begins to blow wild in the wind, Reuben selects some fabric. (T) explain, the wind is making the fabric (move. Reuben enjoys observing the effects of the wind. (a)

Reuben is playing alongside his friend Jowan with the ladders and people, when he has finished (T) Encourages him to tidy up, Reuben picks up all 3 ladders and puts them away in their correct place.

Reuben tells (T) "I want a story", (T) Encourages him to get one. Reuben chooses a book and brings it back. One of his peers wants to share the book too (T) facilitates sharing of opening the flaps, the two boys then take it in turns

Reuben is running with the scissors in a unsafe way (T) explains the safe way to hold the scissors along the metal part. (T) encourages Reuben to hold them the safe way when walking then Reuben understands and tells his peers.

Reuben is making a shopping list and holds the pen with a palm fist grip (T) demonstrates the 3 finger grip. Reuben is confused (T) facilitates putting the 3 finger grip in the Reubens hand and allows him carry on. Reuben is able to keep using the 3 finger grip

(T) is setting up snack bar, (T) Encourages him to Reuben in wording. (T) encourages Reuben to help by saying the snack cards of a friend's join. Reuben (T) set Reuben a challenge to find the correct snack card. Reuben looks at each picture calling out his friends names. Great work Reuben one the snack cards are sorted (T) counts with Reuben 1-13 (T) models language.

Possible Areas For Future Focus:

* Helping to decorate pre-school for christmas
* Take pre-school learning Pack home
* Activities to further develop Reubens fine motor Skills.

Cecie

Learning Journey For _Cecie_   Date _Feb 2019_

Entries should include the initial observation (& assessment), the teaching and the outcome.

Current interests, patterns in learning or information from parents

* Playdough
* Sand
* water play

Cecie wanted to put her coat on (T) encouraged Cecie to do the over the head technique Cecie did this and was happy she did so (photo).

Cecie was watching the rain water coming out of a pipe. She tried to catch it in a bowl but couldn't (T) Showed her another way of placing the bowl. Cecie retried a different bowl and tried (T)'s technique successfully. Photo

Cecie is playing in the sand, she uses a spade to scoop up the sand and then places it in the outside sink. (T) Models language "Scoop" and "tip" Cecie scoops up the sand again bag this time saying "Scoop" and then "tip" as she tips the sand in. (T) communicates that the sand is wet "yes wet" Cecie replies (T) Questions "I wonder how the sand got wet?" "Tip" Cecie replies. photo

Cecie is playing with the playdough "look a heart" (T) Looks "yes you've made a heart" (T) sets a challenge I wonder if you can make a triangle (T) shows Cecie the playdough cutters and Cecie is able to find a triangle. Cecie uses the cutter successfully. (T) gets the rectangle cutter and explains the different shapes (P)

Cecie's top is wet (T) sets Cecie a challenge to get her bag, Cecie returns with no bag (T) supports Cecie to change her top Cecie works hard to be (T) and (T) help when needed. Cecie returns her bag to her peg.

Possible Areas For Future Focus: :)

* Support Cecie to play with other children and build friendships

* Continue to support her with personal care.

Learning Journey For **Liam**..... Date 18/3/19

Entries should include the initial observation (& assessment), the teaching and the outcome.

Current interests, patterns in learning or information from parents
*
*
*

Liam picks up an orange ball outside "Orange" he says holding the ball out for me to see. Ⓣ models language by repeating and extending "yes you've got an orange ball" Liam says "ball ball" and throws the ball into the watertray.

Liam was running inside Ⓣ explained that we use walking feet inside and that if Liam wanted to run he needs to go outside and use running feet

Liam would like to play ī the water Ⓣ explains we need to wear suits Ⓣ shows Liam where the suits are and sets Liam a challenge to take off his boots, Liam attempts and struggles Ⓣ models language and signs "help me" Liam repeats "elp" "ee" Ⓣ supports Liam into his suit and Liam is able to play happily ī the water.

Liam struggles to make a sandcastle without it falling Ⓣ demonstrates how Liam's tower still falls over Ⓣ encourages him to carry on trying. After a few attempts he is successful 'I did it'

Liam is playing in the garden, he watches Ⓣ and his peers throwing balls up in the air. Ⓣ models language "Ready, steady, go" Liam joins in, he picks up a ball Ⓣ models language again "Ready, steady" and leaves a pause "Go" says Liam and throws the ball ...

Possible Areas For Future Focus:
*
*
*

Learning Journey For **Fabian** Date **4.3.19**

Entries should include the initial observation (& assessment), the teaching and the outcome.

Current interests, patterns in learning or information from parents
• Likes to Run, Water Play + Paint. •

Fabian brings a duplo man to T. "dada" he says.
T models language "a man", I wonder where Mummy is and gestures with hands.
Fabian looks around. A while later Fabian finds another duplo person and brings it to T. T "mama".

Fabian hears an aeroplane whilst playing outside, he points to the sky and makes a plane sound. T Models language "Aeroplane, you can hear an aeroplane Fabian"
Fabian points at the plane again "plane" he repeats.

Fabian observes his peer using a paintbrush and water to make marks on the chalk board. T Gets Fabian his own bucket and brush and encourages him to have a go. Fabian begins to make marks on the chalk board and fence. When his water runs out he shows T. T Questions "Do you want more water?" and models sign. Fabian nods and points at the tap. T Facilitates by holding the bucket whilst Fabian pushes the tap to fill it with water. ②

Fabian points at birthday wall, he then gets a chair to stand on for a closer look. T Points to Fabians photo "Fabian".
Fabian then looks around at the family board, he points to his photo, Fabian vocalises as he points to more photos. T Models language and names his peers as he points. T then continues to tell Fabian and peers their months of birth. ①

Possible Areas For Future Focus:
• To use makaton and keep words basic. • "Coat" + "Coat please" with Makaton to build words

* Book Handed Over *

Learning Journey For **hrihaan** Date **March 2019**

Entries should include the initial observation (& assessment), the teaching and the outcome.

Current interests, patterns in learning or information from parents

* settling In
* *
* *

Hrihaan was in the snug he wanted me to buy some cake he gave me some pretend money (T) set a challenge (T) wanted to buy x2 pieces of cake (T) questioned I wonder how many pieces of cake Hrihanna counted

"1, 2 pieces of cake"
(Photo)

Hrihaan was exploring the water area. He holds the turkey baster and is not able to are left Make it work.
(T) Facilitates and Provides explanation
"Squeeze and the water sucks up".
Hrihaan tries by himself several more times before managing it.
(photo)

Hrihaan is Singing a song on the carpet "This little train". (T) Shows him the train and tracks and Sings the song while acting out the words (along the track, up the hill, down the hill). (modeling language). Hrihaan explores the magnets and (T) provides a narrative.

Hrihaan is placing the ball into the hoop (T) wonders if hrihaan can throw it, then sets a challenge to move back and try again. Hrihaan gets the ball in on his second try. (T) claps hrihaan smiles.

Possible Areas For Future Focus:
* Making friends, begin to socialise with others
* Confidence building over time here.
*

Hrihanna was

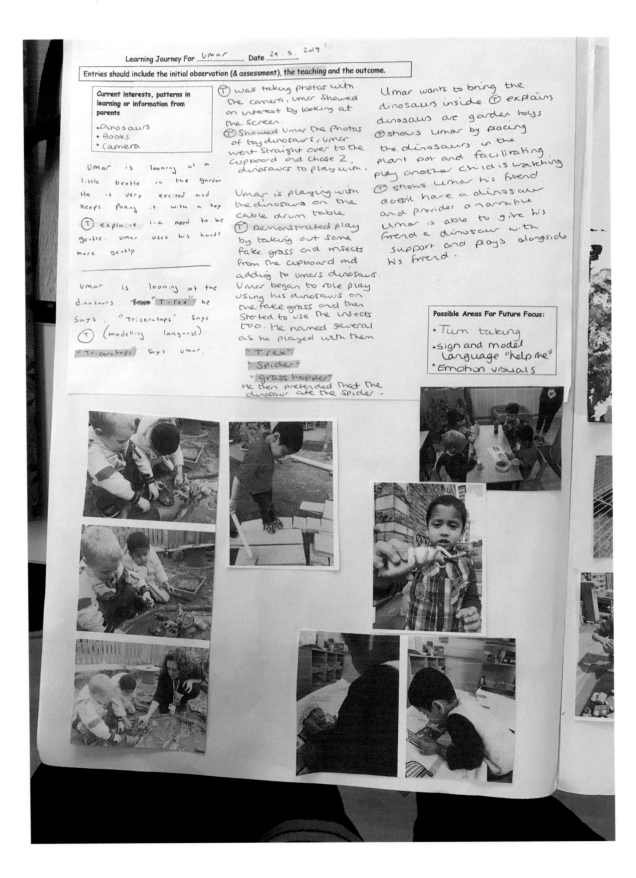

Learning Journey For **Umar**   Date **29.5.2019**

Entries should include the initial observation (& assessment), the teaching and the outcome.

Current interests, patterns in learning or information from parents

* Dinosaurs
* Books
* Camera

Umar is looking at a little beetle in the garden. He is very excited and keeps poking it with a toy. (T) explains the need to be gentle. Umar uses his hands more gently.

Umar is looking at the dinosaurs. ~~Tricas~~ "T-rex" he says. "Triceratops" says (T) (modelling language). "Triceratops" says Umar.

(T) was taking photos with the camera, Umar showed an interest by looking at the screen. (T) showed Umar the photos of toy dinosaurs, Umar went straight over to the cupboard and chose 2 dinosaurs to play with.

Umar is playing with the dinosaurs on the cable drum table. (T) Demonstrated play by taking out some fake grass and insects from the cupboard and adding to Umars dinosaurs. Umar began to role play using his dinosaurs on the fake grass and then started to use the insects too. He named several as he played with them

"T rex"
"Spider"

"grass hopper"
He then pretended that the dinosaur ate the spider.

Umar wants to bring the dinosaurs inside (T) explains dinosaurs are garden toys (T) shows Umar by placing the dinosaurs in the plant pot and facilitating play another child is watching (T) shows Umar his friend doesn't have a dinosaur and provides a narrative Umar is able to give his friend a dinosaur with support and plays alongside his friend.

Possible Areas For Future Focus:

* Turn taking
* sign and model language "help me"
* Emotion visuals

PART II

In action

6 September diary

Home visits

The children who are joining the preschool already visited the setting in July but, for such young children, that can be a distant memory (see Chapter 2 for further information about induction and settling periods). The events that take place in September will be the most powerful in terms of helping the children to feel secure in the preschool environment and therefore keen to stay, even without a parent, eventually. The home visit is a crucial step in this process. It allows staff to see the child in an environment (their home) where they already feel secure and relaxed. They may be shy when staff come to the home but will usually reveal a little of their true character if the visit is relaxed and not rushed. There are the inevitable forms to be completed, but many of these can be done either before or after the home visit. The actual visit should be spent building the first few blocks in the relationship between the preschool and the family and between the staff and the child. Children at this young age do not yet realise that they know different things to other people. So, for example, they have a cat and they assume that everyone knows that they have a cat. Or there are new twin babies in the house and they assume everyone knows about this because they know about it. This aspect of theory of mind is fascinating and can help practitioners understand why the home visit is so important. The child believes that whatever they know, the staff at the preschool know too. So, when they talk about 'Tiggy' or 'Nonny', they will assume that the staff know what this refers to. The home visit can help fill in these pieces of the jigsaw and help the relationship between the staff and children to grow.

The visit will also reveal some aspects of the child's experiences in the home. For example, there might be a garden, piles of children's books, tubs of play dough and construction toys, and the television might not be on, or there might be no access to a garden, a large television which is on constantly and electronic tablets in evidence, but no books or toys. When observing these things, the staff are not being judgmental, but the information will help them to know how to interact with the child, what experiences will be familiar to them and where they might need support. Once the family begins to trust the staff and they realise that the staff want to work in partnership with the parents and in the best interests of the child, then they begin to ask for advice and support if they need it. Equally, they begin to feel confident to tell staff about any specific achievements of their child, anything that they have found that is particularly successful with their child, and they can support the staff in understanding special words or sounds that their child might use.

The visit is also a good opportunity to see how the parents/carers interact with their child and how the child responds, how confident their speech is (whether English or not) and how behaviour is handled. Again, this is not about judging anyone; rather, it is about getting to know what a child is used to and how they respond to familiar adults.

The staff will take a few resources with them, and these again provide opportunities to observe the children and see how they respond, and they can then use this knowledge once the children arrive at the preschool.

Induction

Stay and play sessions

All families are invited to spend time at the setting with their child. For some children, just one or two visits will be enough to give the child enough confidence to be ready to be left without a parent/carer. For other children, the presence of a familiar adult will be essential for much longer before the child will feel confident enough to remain on their own. It is important to be flexible in these arrangements and to allow parents to stay as long as necessary. Equally, if parents are trying to leave their child too soon, staff should explain that by rushing this process, they will be creating longer term problems. (See Chapter 2 for further discussion of this subject.)

During a stay and play session, Eymen had time to explore the resources on offer and the animals were an immediate source of interest for him. The resources are organised to be visible and accessible to the children. Therefore, even though Eymen had no English, he was able to find what he needed without having to ask an adult. He was also given the time and freedom to move objects from one area to another, resulting in this arrangement of animals on the table.

The induction has been successful

It is clear that the induction processes at Staple Hill Stars have been successful this year. The evidence for this is seen in the children. The vast majority of them have settled very quickly, and by the end of September, nearly all are showing high levels of well-being and involvement. The staff have adapted the strategies according to the needs of each child.

Some strategies that proved successful this year were as follows:

- Parents stayed for several sessions.
- Staff printed photos of mum or dad for the child to keep with them during a session.
- Children brought in a transition object which they either kept in their pocket or which was placed in view somewhere in the room.
- Parents left the room for very short periods and gradually extended this.
- Some children kept their pacifier for short periods.
- Some children were carried and cuddled.
- Some children needed a short distraction.

For example, when Daisy was distressed, the staff gave her a dummy from home and carried her for a while. They also showed her pictures from home and explained that Mummy would be back very soon. The time that mum left the room was gradually increased. Once her emotions had been acknowledged, and Daisy had been comforted and reassured, the staff then distracted Daisy with her favourite activity of playing with the dolls. Over a few sessions, Daisy relaxed, enjoyed herself and learnt that Mummy would return. Once her well-being improved, so too did her levels of involvement. Two-year-olds will take a few experiences to know and understand that mum will come back. So it is important for parents to leave for short periods at first and then return so that the child will begin to understand this concept.

Establishing expectations

During any stay and play session or during their first proper sessions at the preschool, the parents are encouraged to help to teach their children the expectations (again, see Chapter 2 for further discussion of this). In the two photos that follow, we see Eymen's mum, who is investing time to help her son to settle. While he is engrossed in an activity, she is observing and just 'being present'. This is allowing him to have positive experiences in the preschool without worrying that Mummy is going to leave. After he has finished painting, his mum is showing him how to operate the tap and soap dispenser so that he will be able to wash his hands independently in future.

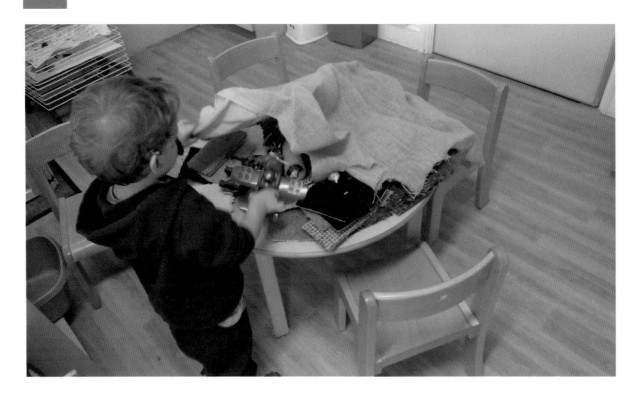

Reuben was confident to stay without a parent quite quickly. However, he still needed support during the settling period. On one occasion, an adult encouraged him to explore the animals. This short interaction led on to a long period of focused play as Reuben transported more and more resources to the table and then enveloped them in a large piece of fabric.

The adults in the room (staff and parents) are also on hand to show the children how to use the snack area. The children need to learn to wash their hands before snack, where to get the cups and plates from and where to put them when they have finished. Adults not only 'teach' all these routines and expectations, but, if at all possible, they sit and talk to the children when they are having their snack.

Another critical focus at this early stage in the year is to **promote friendships** amongst the group.

In the photo here, we see that Asude had created this eating area. Staff observed that when other children came near it, she held up her hand and said "No!" An adult then encouraged her to move her game to the sand pit so that more children could join the game. With limited English, a lot of signing and gesturing was needed, but eventually Asude moved her game and was then happy to have some friends to play with.

Tidying up is another big focus early in the year (and all year long with this age group). The staff all know that the expectation is that **'when the children have finished playing with something, then they put it back where it belongs'.** The organisation of the resources supports this with clear and obvious 'homes' for each resource. Also, because the children get the resources out, they know where to put them back.

For example, on one occasion, Mia was about to leave the play dough table, and an adult reminded her about putting the things away before she left. She remembered how to compare the shapes of the objects to the shadows on the shelves and was able to tidy everything quickly, as the photo here shows.

The staff have agreed that the children will wear aprons in the water. Despite a strong attraction to water play – both indoors and outside, Asude resisted wearing an apron. The staff were confident that Asude did not have a fear of aprons and nor did she get distressed when asked to put one on. She just refused and walked away. However, when Eliza was playing at the indoor water tray and Asude wanted to join her, it was Eliza who managed to persuade Asude to put an apron on. Thus we see how even the youngest children can become the teachers for their peers.

The outdoor area is available all the time and therefore the staff have agreed that the indoor areas will be quiet. If the children want to shout or run, then they are reminded to go into the garden. The arrangement of the room also supports the quiet atmosphere. For example, the carpet area seen here, is 'protected' by the storage units and panels that surround it. This means that children do not run across the carpet – they have to go around – and therefore children can play and build without fear of being disrupted.

While the indoor areas remain quieter, the outdoor area can be where the louder, bigger and messier play can take place.

Enjoyable experiences help children to settle and to want to come into preschool

The following photos show a snapshot of the hundreds of activities that occurred in the preschool during September. In each case, the children have selected where to play and which resources to use. The involvement is high – proving that the provision is meeting the needs and interests of the children. This deep involvement will ensure that the children are keen to return to preschool each day.

Here we see Jowan in the creative area – experimenting with paint at the easel and later using the glue to attach items to a sheet of paper.

Playing outside in all the autumn weathers brings further, possibly, new and enjoyable experiences to the children. For example, on a very windy day, the staff demonstrate how the fabric behaves in the wind. Notice how two children have joined Hayley balancing on the climbing apparatus.

Even in the pouring rain, the children have the option to go outdoors. Although some resources are not used in the rain (fabric, blocks, paper and so on), many areas and resources are still in use. Bubbles are a source of fascination for young children, whatever the weather.

Being able to play outdoors in all weathers is exactly what 2-year-olds yearn to do. Their deep involvement and high well-being are all the evidence we need to know that this is meeting their emotional and developmental needs. The environment and resources offer experiences that many would not access at home, and the large construction resources are one such example of this.

Friendships begin to emerge

These three photos show a new friendship that developed in the early weeks of the term between Annabelle and Jowan.

Babies and young children learn so much by observing the other people around them and mimicking their actions, words and gestures. Adults working with the 2-year-olds will learn very quickly that they have to be very careful about what a child sees them do. For example, if an adult decides to throw a spade back into the basket rather than walking over and placing it there, then within minutes, there will be spades being thrown all over the place. Just as they learn from watching the adults, they also learn by watching the other children. With this friendship established, we see Annabelle developing confidence with climbing, which might not have happened so quickly without the role model of her friend.

Eliza has been in this room for a few months already – she is clear about the expectations and is confident and settled in the environment. There are many advantages of having a wide range of ages and experiences, and next we can see two examples. There are advantages both for the younger children (who have extra 'teachers') and also for the older children whose self-esteem is boosted by being able to support younger children. Also when one person teachers another (in this case a slightly older child), they reinforce their own skill/knowledge in doing so.

With more experience of the preschool, Eliza is able to help other children. For example she can be seen here helping Fabian to put on a hat and demonstrating to Eymen how to take turns holding a cup and pouring water for each other at the water tray.

Teaching of 'next steps' in the moment begins

These two children were struggling to use the pulley effectively. An adult explained that it might be easier to walk backwards and then pointed out how the bucket went "up, up, up" as the child walked backwards. Then as the child walked forwards, the adult pointed out that the bucket went "down, down, down". The children were then able to use the equipment successfully and began to repeat the words themselves as they played. The joy on Sammy's face tells us all we need to know. This 'teaching' in this moment was exactly appropriate – pitched at the correct level for these two children in this moment.

Here, Kaz has joined two girls at the play dough table. The girls were trying to make long 'sausage' shapes as they had seen another child do. Kaz modelled how to roll the play dough between two palms, narrating quietly as she did so "two hands together, roll backwards and forwards". The girls were then able to create their own 'sausage' shapes.

A group of children were using the instruments outside, and the two tapping sticks became very popular. When more children wanted to use them, the adult explained that there were other sticks in the sand area and encouraged the children to try those. Reuben was clearly very satisfied with the sound that these sticks could make as he tapped them together. The adult then began singing children's names and demonstrated how to tap the syllables on the sticks. The children joined in – beginning to hear the rhythm of names, but probably more importantly, learning the names of their new friends.

As September comes to an end, it is clear that the year is off to a great start. The children are all settled, with high well-being and beginning to show deep levels of involvement. The expectations are being established so that each child will continue to feel secure and happy in the environment. The staff are exhausted, as is always the case at this early stage of the year. However, they can already see how their hard work is paying off. They already have strong, trusting relationships with the children so that they know how to interact with each child. They can see that the way they have organised the environment is working superbly in terms of supporting the interests of each child and also in terms of supporting their independence. The children have settled and the staff are beginning to teach 'in the moment', observing progress and development occurring constantly.

7 October diary

Initial assessments

Staple Hill Stars Pre-school have opted to use the assessment and tracking tool designed by Early Excellence (EExAT) – see Chapter 5 for further details. For initial assessments, EExAT is clear that the children should be settled before any assessment is made. Their system uses the Leuven Scales of Well-Being and Involvement to determine when a child is 'settled'. Once a child is demonstrating good levels of well-being, then we can feel confident that they are feeling more secure and relaxed in the setting. The rationale is that if a child has not settled, then there is little point trying to make any assessments, as they will not be a true reflection of the child. A child who is still anxious, upset or worried, for example, is not going to be able to demonstrate their true capabilities. They will remain in 'fight or flight' mode and will not be relaxed enough to show what they are capable of. However, once a child is showing good well-being, the system encourages staff to look at levels of involvement. Once a child is showing deep levels of involvement, this indicates increased 'brain activity' and learning. Therefore, if a 'baseline' is to actually reflect the 'starting point' of a child, then it is important to carry out these 'on-entry' assessments as soon as possible after a child has settled. The assessments are done purely based on the adults' observations of the children – meaning what they observe the children doing in the setting. There is no requirement that any of these observations are recorded on paper. Staff knowledge is the main source of any evidence that is used to make any assessments – be that for 'on-entry' or later in the year. For each child, once they are 'settled', then the staff will try to complete their 'on-entry' assessment within the next two weeks. The EExAT tracker is simple and quick to complete, with clear, age-related statements to consider. There is no need to make 'best-fit' judgements. The system uses a few key indicators of typical progress, recognising that, if a child is developing typically for their age in these aspects of development, then they are 'on track' in more general terms. It is not necessary or possible to assess every tiny aspect of development. It is preferable to use a system, such as EExAT, which will highlight any child who is not developing typically but, equally, can be completed very quickly and accurately for all children so that staff can focus their attention back onto interacting – that is, teaching. By the end of October, all the 'on-entry' assessments have been completed for the children who joined the nursery in September. The tracker gives cohort summary information and can therefore be used to track cohort progress at intervals throughout the year.

First cycle of focus children begins

In Chapter 5, you can also read about the focus child system, which is a way of keeping the record keeping to a manageable level.

> **All staff are interacting with all children, but they will just be recording significant interactions with a few 'focus children' each week, along with 'Wow!' moments for any child.**

The examples of events that are shown in this chapter are just a snippet of the events that occurred in October. Some are from the focus children, and some are from other children. There are several examples of completed focus child sheets at the end of Chapter 5. During their first 'focus week', **the parents of the focus children are invited to stay in** the preschool and to observe how the setting runs. This allows staff to demonstrate how they interact and 'teach' the children while they are playing at activities that they have chosen themselves. This is often very reassuring for parents. They learn that although their child might be playing in the sand all morning, the staff will join the child in the sand, observe them for a while and then interact with them to support their development, without causing them any stress, by allowing them to continue with the play that interests them.

Children become settled and can then explore

The next picture below captures the moment when Daisy first showed deep involvement in her play. This not only indicates her involvement but is evidence that her levels of well-being are higher, allowing her to relax and explore. The activity of a 'picnic' was enough of an enticement to make this possible. Once children have one positive experience, then this is lodged and remembered – making the next positive experience much easier to occur.

The picture here shows how some children have now settled completely and are playing independently, while others still need the reassurance of a cuddle. In the photo that follows, we see how Kerry is able to both comfort a child on her lap and interact with the children at the play dough table. This experience will also allow Shaydon to watch as other children explore and have a positive experience, which will eventually entice him to become involved.

Children begin to use the new/unfamiliar resources

Reuben has been exploring the various loose parts and objects in the garden. He had created a vehicle with the cable drum and steering wheel. After playing for a while, he went and fetched a piece of hose-pipe to use as a seat belt, which can be seen in the photo that follows. This sort of creativity and original thinking is a demonstration of the innate drive to learn that is within all children. It also shows that with fewer, versatile resources, the creativity is essential and is therefore maintained and developed. When children are constantly given access to resources which only have one possible use, then their creativity and thinking skills are not required, not 'pushed' into use and therefore not developed. So, for example, a commercially bought car that a child can ride in will give them different experiences, but it does not demand the critical or creative thinking that Reuben has displayed. Similarly, when staff in settings spend ages creating a vehicle and include all the seats, doors, seat belts etc., it may look wonderful and appealing, but again, it is taking away the thought processes from the children.

Annabelle can be seen in the photo that follows, exploring the creative area and, in particular, the felt-tip pens. Some children at this age have not yet found their dominant hand, and it is crucial that they are feeling secure so that they can explore everything on offer at this stage. Here Annabelle is experimenting with using two pens at once and has just realised that one pen still has the lid on. Such moments are powerful learning opportunities. An adult could step in and remove the lid, but this would limit the learning. It is far better to give the child time to process what is happening and to resolve the situation herself. Imagine the steps of thought that this will entail as she realises what is happening, puts one pen down, removes the lid from the other, picks up the first one again, manoeuvres both pens back into position and eventually manages to make marks with both. These tiny moments of concentration and effort are happening constantly with children of this age, and it is easy to overlook their potential, or indeed, to overlook them altogether.

In the next two pictures, we see Betsy as she masters the outdoor tap. This tap is incredibly stiff and hard to use. Betsy has persevered with encouragement and commentary from the staff.

> **At this point, with some sustained effort, she has succeeded and the delight on her face is clear. It is this sort of experience that builds a child's resilience.**

Again, an adult could have pressed the tap for her, and that might be appropriate for other children. However, the staff have realised that Betsy is strong enough to do this herself, and they also know that this sort of experience is exactly what young children need in order to further grow their resilience. It is definitely a challenge for the child but one that, with a bit of effort, she can succeed at. If she were not strong enough or tall enough, then the adults would have stepped in to help.

> **Young children do not need to be put into situations where they continually struggle and fail, as each time this happens, a little more of their resilience is chipped away.**

Equally, they do not need resources, experiences or activities that are too easy, where no effort is needed, as this again does not develop resilience. They need experiences exactly like this – as simple as turning on the tap – but a tap that is stiff and hard to use.

Expectations continue to be demonstrated

Some children have already begun to tidy up independently, and others still need reminding. The setting has adopted the approach that the children will tidy up after they have finished playing with a resource or in an area. This is not always as simple as it sounds when other children are still using the resources, but as often as possible, the children are reminded to put away the things that they have been using before moving to another area. In this way, the room and garden remain relatively tidy and attractive for other children. Thus, in the next picture, Fabian is being shown how to use the dustpan and brush next to the sand tray.

Huge age range is evident

In a 2–3 room, the age range of the children can be as much as 23 months – with a child aged 24 months starting at the setting at a time when the oldest child is 47 months. In other preschools, where the children are all together, this age range could be even greater. Mixed-aged classes do exist in schools but are not the norm, and the older the children become, the age differences become less relative to their ages. There are enormous benefits to having mixed ages. Older children are superb role models, supporting younger children, modelling language, play, skills, routines etc. This also boosts their self-esteem and well-being and ensures a culture of empathy is developed from this young age. However, it also has its challenges. Some resources and activities are challenging and engaging for all ages, but others are not. The 'sand kitchen', shown here with a 24-month-old child, is an example of an area of provision that appeals to all ages and is 'safe' yet engaging for all ages.

Equally, the pipes, guttering and loose parts appeal to and engage all children. The advantages of the mixed ages are exemplified in the photo that follows, where an older child has constructed this series of 'runs'. The activity of building this has been a challenge for Hudson, but he has succeeded (thus developing his resilience), and it is now possible for younger children to be engaged and challenged by the activity of finding a ball or a vehicle to send down the various runs.

With the children becoming more settled, it is possible for the staff to spend slightly longer periods interacting with individual children. They also know them so well now that they know how to interact and challenge each child. They know which children can 'take a joke', which children still need reminders and reassurance that the expectations are set and will not shift etc. Most importantly, because they know each child so well, they know exactly how to move their learning on. They know exactly the right level of challenge and 'teaching' to use with each individual child, and they know that this is unique to each child. For example, the staff know that Asude is often engaged in mark-making in all areas and with various materials. They have observed how she is able to draw recognisable figures and assigns labels to each 'mummy, daddy' etc. She has drawn people with paint, with water on the blackboard outdoors, with a stick in the sand and with felt pens on paper. Thus, when she approached Hayley and indicated that she would like to use Hayley's pen, this was the perfect opportunity to facilitate an effective grip and to encourage Asude to draw in her special book. Asude was keen to use the pen, and Hayley knew that she was physically able to hold the pen in a pincer grip. This combination then constituted a teachable moment in which the conditions were exactly right for the child to be receptive to the teaching and for it to 'stick' – i.e. for the learning to take place and the 'next step' to be achieved.

As October comes to an end, the staff are exhausted, but they can see that the children have settled, routines are established, relationships are growing and the children are making wonderful progress. Their hard work and commitment are paying off, and the year promises to be challenging but rewarding for everyone.

November diary

Toilet training

By November all the children are settled in the preschool, and therefore staff are able to make decisions about how, when and if to interact with each child. The decision to tackle toilet training with any child requires just such understanding. With this particular task, it is an on-going debate as to how many children to train at one time and how to go about this. The staff recognise that this is an important aspect of child development at this age but also wish to maintain the ability to interact with all children in all areas of development. If the toilet training is too time-consuming for too many staff, then other areas of development can be overlooked to some extent. Another important aspect of this work is to ensure that the parents/carers are in agreement and are willing to adopt the same strategies and approach at home. There are 40 children on role, with a maximum of 20 in each session in the 2–3 room at Staple Hill. Staff try to ensure that they are toilet-training no more than two children in each session. This would be in addition to the children who are out of nappies but still need reminders. By the end of the year, there are usually only three or four children going up to the next room (for the year before Reception) who are still in nappies.

Cold, wet weather

November is often the month when the weather changes to become much wetter and colder, and in the 2–3 room, this brings extra work for staff as they strive to ensure that children remain warm and dry without restricting access to outdoors. It has been an on-going wish to have improved outdoor wet-weather clothing at the preschool, and this year the new clothing is going to be purchased. However, the new clothing has not yet arrived, and so the challenges remain and staff have to be extra vigilant. The children already have access to the stock of wellington boots that have been available for a while. For now, they are wearing their normal outdoor coats with waterproof aprons over the top. This is far from ideal, and the search for the perfect outdoor wear has become a priority.

Scissors

For many children in the 2–3 room, the access to scissors is a new and enticing experience. When young children are given permission to use 'real' tools which they have observed parents or older children using, they are often intrigued and keen to master the new skill. A pair of scissors is one such tool, and these have been made available in many areas of the preschool – both indoors and outside. The next three photos show just how appealing this is for young children. However, it is the level of involvement which is the indicator that this is something valuable in terms of learning, as the children focus and 'push' their brain to develop and allow them to succeed. The staff have provided various types of scissors in different areas – so, for example, there are plastic scissors in the play dough area. Play dough is a good material with which to practice cutting skills, as it succumbs easily. This means that the child can practice the necessary hand movements to operate the scissors without having to worry too much about the angle of the play dough to the scissors, as is the case with paper.

Asude began cutting masking tape that was held taut by being stretched between two furniture units – as if taking part in a 'grand opening'. Other children then copied this play, and this proved another way of facilitating the cutting process. The tape was held still, meaning that the children could concentrate on maneuvering the scissors without having to also hold the tape still. The picture of Leon here shows a common stage that children go through with scissors, using two hands to achieve the open-close motion.

Adults will often interact with children when they are attempting to use new tools or equipment. According to their knowledge of the child, they will choose how or whether to offer support, so they might give verbal instruction, a practical demonstration, encouragement or, as seen in the photo below, facilitation. This photo shows how the adult is doing one part of the process, that of holding the paper in the correct position and at the correct angle and keeping it taut, so that Shaydon can just concentrate on the hand control of opening and closing the scissors whilst keeping the blades in contact with the paper. The 'mirroring' motion with the left hand is typical at this age and shows deep involvement and 'brain activity'.

For some children, who prefer to be outdoors, it is helpful to offer these experiences and resources in the garden as well. The next photo shows the final stage of mastering the scissors – Ava is holding the paper with one hand and the scissors with the other, managing the hand movements to open and close the scissors and keeping the paper and scissors in the right position and at an effective angle. The brain power required is immense, and repetition will be required to 'hard-wire' this learning in the brain.

Friendships and play in groups

Many children in the 2–3 room play alongside their peers, but occasionally, and more often as they get older, more social play becomes apparent. The next photo shows one such occasion. Each child in this photo has a different first language, but by combining the use of gestures, Makaton and some English, they are able to play together. Even though the staff were not absolutely clear about what the play was about, they recognised the deep levels of involvement as the indicator that this was a powerful experience for the children. It is this willingness to 'let go' of some of the control that is so refreshing in this setting. The staff understand that they do not need to know and understand everything that is happening. They trust that the children want to be deeply involved and also understand that when that is the case, there is brain activity and learning happening. The adult agenda is put aside to allow the children to lead. Sometimes, as with this play, the adults were not clear as to the purpose of the play, but they valued it for the well-being and involvement that it supported in the children.

The water play is another area where there are often groups of children playing together. Sometimes this is 'copying' and 'mirroring', but at other times, the first elements of cooperation are seen. Initially this involves taking turns at the tap, putting water down the pipes or using a particularly popular boat or other resource. Gradually, when a child needs help with something, they begin to ask other children for help, or other children begin to help without being asked. So, for example, one child will operate the tap and another will hold their bucket underneath the water to fill it up. Or one child needs more than one container of water to 'push' the duck down the pipe, and two children will end up saying "Ready, steady, go!" and pouring the water down together to achieve success.

Indoors, the role play and carpet areas are often the first areas where this sort of more social and cooperative play is noticed. The train for example is a resource that can be used by a group of children, but they often need adult guidance and support with this to begin with. The adult is nearby to ensure that, if one child has built a section of track, then other children need to be aware and respectful of this. However, they also come to realise that the track can be longer and more interesting when more than one child is helping to build it. The bridges or raised sections are particularly challenging, but some children can then be recognised and encouraged to use their building skill to make the track more interesting for other children to use.

The block play is similar – both indoors and outdoors – children are beginning to see that they can build structures alone, but it can also be different and possibly better to build with others. The next two photos show this happening indoors and outside. The potential frustrations that can occur when one child doesn't follow the ideas of another will need sensitive adult guidance and interaction so that the children learn to interact with each other. This will ensure that, going forward, they will be able to play and negotiate without the need for an adult to be there. Thus the adults model phrases for the children to use with each other: "Wait a minute, I just want to put this on first"; "We need to put this one here"; "Please don't take that block, I am using it"; "Can we try this first?" They will also be there to encourage children to look at other children and to notice the emotions of the other children. This will encourage empathy and hopefully ensure more cooperative play going forward. So, for example, they might say "Look, Charlie looks sad because he was using that plank"; "Look, Taz is angry because you knocked his bridge over." They will then encourage the child to think of a way to sort out the problem.

Some interests persist over time

As a young child, I had a doll at home named Janet. When her eye got damaged, she was sent off to the 'dolls' hospital' to be repaired.

I remember waiting anxiously for her to return. I also remember taking her to the Co-op in a pram, carrying her to the park, feeding her, bathing her, dressing her etc. This interest in babies and young children has persisted my whole life. The interests that children display at this age might persist, they might not. However, we must trust that children will choose to play with the things that interest and engage them. Within this play, they will be motivated to try new things and to challenge themselves. Umar has shown an interest in the animals since his very first visit to the preschool, and now that he is settled, the interest is persisting. The photos that follow show him using the toy animals in different ways – and in both he is combining the animals with other resources. In the first, he is enacting how cars and animals move, and in the second, he is using the paint to see the 'prints' that the animals' feet produce.

Staff interact continuously

The previous photos show children, in groups or individually, but mainly without an adult. However, please remember that the adults are nearby, observing and looking for moments when they can interact and make a difference. The photos that follow show some examples of this. Although the children are settled, they are still very young and need reminders about the expectations in the setting. The next photo shows Kaz doing just this – "Remember to hang the apron back on the hook. Look, there is a spare hook here."

Children at this age are keen to be independent but sometimes need help with part of a process. For example, even though most of the children can now put their coats on independently, staff facilitate the process of doing up the zips by helping with the bottom part of the zip and then encouraging the child to do the rest – as shown in the photo on the left. In other situations, staff model how to use resources and then the children are able to complete the process themselves. Cutting bananas, as seen here, is one such example.

In the next photo, Anna can be seen interacting with Alexis-Rose at the play dough table. The 'trust' between adult and child can be felt by noticing the body language. This does not happen by accident. The staff have spent time getting to know the children so that they know how and when to interact with them. The children have now learnt that the adults can be trusted and therefore will approach them for support, for a chat, for comfort, for help. In this example, Alexis-Rose wanted to make 'sausages and peas', and Anna has modelled the techniques to produce the necessary shapes.

In this example, the child was totally in control of the interaction and the adult was responding sensitively. On some occasions, the adults notice possibilities and will make the decision to impose slightly more guidance within an interaction. This might be to explain or demonstrate something new or unfamiliar. It might be to introduce the children to an experience that is relevant in the particular moment. Staff moving to a more spontaneous way of working often worry about the need to introduce the children to new experiences, and of course this is still possible and desirable. However, it is far more powerful if it can be done in the moment when children are already interested in something, already giving their attention to something, already keen to find out more. The next two photos are examples of this type of interaction. In the first we see Kaz explaining to the children about the mini-beast on the leaf, reassuring them that it will not hurt them, modelling how to hold it safely, wondering what it might like to eat and so on. In the second photo, we see how Kaz has been working jointly with the children, demonstrating and scaffolding how to build a complex structure with the blocks and loose parts. This is the sort of construction that the children might not 'discover' themselves but is exactly at the level of complexity to mean that they will be intrigued by the process but able to complete it again themselves on another occasion.

The November weather has been wet and cold, but the staff and children have continued to play and learn both indoors and outside, overcoming challenges and supporting each other. As November comes to an end, the individual children have become a 'group' with its own mini-culture and character. It is a group that is lively, caring, happy and curious – just the characteristics we need for children to remain the life-long learners that they were at birth. As individuals, many are becoming interested in their own learning and development as well as the learning and development of their peers. Their 'special books' (see Chapter 5 for an explanation of these) are a source of great interest. The final photo in this chapter shows two girls studying their special books and talking about the photos and all the things that they have done in the first few months of preschool. Their enthusiasm when looking back at their books was a delight to witness and a clear indication that their time in this preschool will be remembered fondly. They are clearly very happy – meaning they have high well-being – and each photo shows how they have been deeply involved in numerous events and activities over the past few months. The remainder of the year will deliver further opportunities and experiences for them to become involved with and to reflect upon.

9 December diary

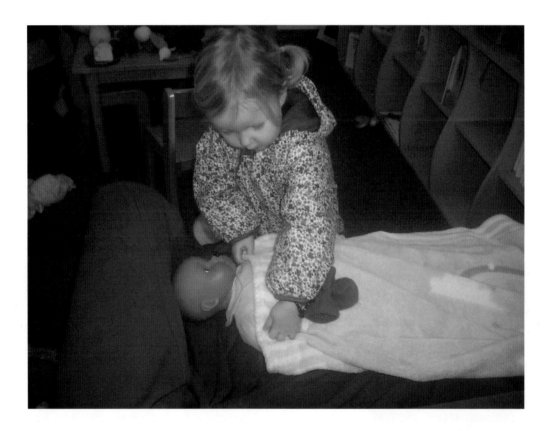

Focus children

By the end of December, most children in the 2–3 room will have had two cycles when they were a focus child. For children who are already 3, then they would just have had one completed cycle in this autumn term (from September to December). It is a constant juggle to keep enough adults in the setting, and the extra challenge comes about because the legal ratios change when a child turns 3, and the funding changes too. For the children aged 2, the ratios in England at this time are 1–4, but as soon as they turn 3, it drops to 1–8. This is one reason why settings have ended up reducing the frequency at which a child is a focus child. For children over 3, it is once per term (or roughly 10% of the group). For children under 3, it is once per half-term (or roughly 20% of the group). With fewer staff, it is more important that they are spending their time interacting with children rather than recording interactions. However, it is also the case that children under 3 are developing at the most rapid pace that will ever happen in their lifetime. The progress that they make in the space of a month can be dramatic. The team at the preschool therefore recognise that it is valuable to get more frequent 'snapshots' of the children at this age, and therefore the children aged under 3 are focus children once per half-term. The team at Staple Hill decided to do the second cycle of focus children with the 2-year-olds, but they did not meet with the parents again. Rather, they sent the focus sheet home and had more informal discussions with the parents about these.

End of term assessments

The staff are now familiar with the Early Excellence tracking system that they are using and were able to complete the end of term assessments quickly. These showed that all but a few children have made 'better than typical' progress.

Home visits and other arrangements

With term time settings, and with other settings too, it is often the case that there is a new influx of children in January. At Staple Hill in 2019, there were indeed new children due to start at the preschool in the new year. Therefore, the staff arranged for sessions when the children could come and visit with their parents in December, and they were visited at home as well. So their introduction and settling procedures were the same as for the children in September.

Christmas and other celebrations/festivals/special events

As with everything else, staff take the lead from the children with regard to the introduction of Christmas. However, it is up to the adults to discuss and agree as a team how to develop the inevitable interest and excitement.

This year several of the focus children had photos of a Christmas tree at home and were animated talking about their tree and the decorations. The staff agreed that they would like to put up a tree in class. With the discovery that there were very few decorations, the staff suggested that children could make their own! The children were deeply involved in making decorations and in decorating the tree. The staff decided that they would remove the decorations at the end of each day so that the children could have the experience of re-decorating it each morning when they arrived.

Many of the photos from home reflect religious, traditional or just 'regular' events. In many cases the children are simply aware that they wore special clothes or that they had a special meal. What is important at this age is that all the children feel comfortable about sharing their experiences. Any setting develops its own 'culture' in this way because it is made up of many unique children, each with unique life experiences. One of the most important things we can do as practitioners is to develop within the group a culture of respect, acceptance, interest and enjoyment of the diversity. Staff should not, therefore, become stressed and anxious trying to make sure that they mention and celebrate every cultural event during the year. The details and facts about each child's culture are important to them – the atmosphere in which they are received in the preschool is important to everyone.

This year at Staple Hill, the staff team agreed that they should have craft materials available for the children to use if they wished to make a card for anyone. In the event, every child did opt to make something. In other years this has not been the case, and if a child did not want to make a card for a parent, then the staff would explain this to the parent and also explain that they would not force a child to do this activity if they did not want to. The next three photos show the buzz of activity at the creative table as the cards were made.

Many children started to make cards for each other, and some children brought cards in from home. One child mentioned the need for a post box, and the creation of this was challenging and engaging for several children.

The next discussion amongst the team was the idea of a party, and again the team agreed that they did want the children to have this experience. The event was kept 'low key' to avoid over-excitement but did involve some games, dancing, music and a visit from Father Christmas. The event was a bit stressful for some children and also incredibly hard work and demanding for the staff. For some, it reminded them of how the preschool used to be run all the time. In particular, the party meant that staff had to control and move children to particular areas at particular times and get them to do particular activities all together. This was indeed how the setting used to be run all the time before they moved to a more child-led approach, with uninterrupted free-flow play. So, although the party was enjoyable for some and a new (if stressful) experience for others, the staff were relieved when it was over and normal routines could be resumed.

10 January diary

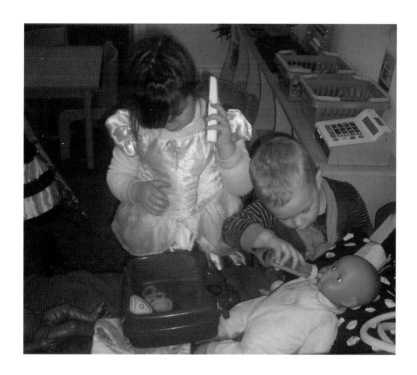

New children

At Staple Hill, many new children often begin at the preschool in January; 2019 was no exception, and the new children brought a change in dynamics, with the youngest children (some of just 24 months) needing a lot of adult support during their first days and weeks in the preschool. As with all new children, the parents were encouraged to stay for as long as they wished, and the decision about when to leave their child was made jointly with the staff. With many adults spending extra time with the new and young children, most of the older children were able to cope with less attention, and this independence was great to see. Some of them even took on the role of supporting the new children and showing them how to do things in the preschool. Here we see Asude supporting Kayla (aged 25 months) to walk along a plank. The staff would not normally hold a child's hand to climb, but the important thing to note in this instance is the empathy and support that an older child is showing to a younger child.

A few of the older children found the changes more difficult to cope with, and their emotions translated into 'interesting' behaviour. They began to test the boundaries – wandering away from the snack table while still eating, 'forgetting' to tidy an area when they had finished playing and so on. The adults had to work extremely hard in these weeks and often felt like they were just 'fire-fighting' rather than having time for quality interactions. By the end of the month, however, they were feeling more positive, with the new children settled and the atmosphere feeling calmer once again.

Reviewing the environment

Waterproof clothing: For several months, the staff have been aware of the need for improved outdoor waterproof clothing. In January the new clothing arrived with waterproof dungarees and coats. There is already a stock of boots at the preschool, and now the children can be completely kitted out. This means that they are able to remain completely dry even when kneeling or sitting in very wet sand, when playing with the water outdoors and when the rain comes down. Although quite an expensive investment, this can transform the experiences of the children in a setting and can ease the workload of the staff.

Woodwork: The staff have been discussing the fact that some of the older children are not always as deeply involved as they were previously. The staff are aware that some of this is due to the fact that new children have started and the staff have not been able to spend quality time with some children for a few weeks. However, they are also keen to introduce a few more experiences into the provision, and one suggestion is to have a wood-work bench. There is already a woodwork area in the garden for the 3- and 4-year-olds, but the staff in the 2–3 room feel that some children would benefit greatly if this was added to their provision too. There are obvious concerns because some of the children are only 24 months old. However, my experience has shown me that very young children are attracted to the woodwork area but quickly realise that it is too difficult for them, and then they lose interest. They might return at intervals, and eventually they will be strong enough and physically developed enough to achieve success, and then they will remain and participate. This sort of behaviour is typical and is seen in all aspects of the provision. Children will naturally choose to do the things that are challenging enough but not impossible. They will not choose the 'easy' option (as it will not engage them), but equally they will not choose something that is way beyond their ability (as this will just frustrate them). They choose things that, perhaps with a little support, they can persevere at and succeed at. Thus, one child, on a particular day, at their particular stage of development, will persevere to peel their own satsuma, put on their own coat and put the train track together but will avoid holding a pencil or using the scissors. We must trust children to make these choices and believe that they will continue to challenge themselves as their development progresses. As a result of these discussions, a woodwork bench has been ordered, and its arrival is eagerly awaited.

Role play

The children have been engaged in various role play scenarios this month, and in particular, three have been recurrent and often are in the 2–3 room. These are hairdressing, doctors and caring for babies. The domestic role play of cooking occurs daily, with trips to the hairdresser or the doctor supplementing this play.

The baby care has been the most prevalent and will continue throughout the year. It is something that the children might be experiencing at home or when with their friends. But for many it is a fascination that appears from the age of about 10 months and persists (in some cases into adulthood). With children in a setting, it is important to have enough 'babies' so that 'sharing' is not always necessary. Children at the age of 2 or 3 have strong and immediate desires, and if they were at home, they would not have to share very often. With older children, it is possible to explain and to encourage more turn taking and so on, but with the 2-year-olds, it is less stressful and more rewarding to have enough resources to minimise the need for sharing.

With this in mind, the preschool has purchased extra doctor role play kits so that a few children can all be the doctor at the same time. The doctor role play is also something that children at this age can take part in very well because they have first-hand experience of the doctors. For parents with a first baby, a high temperature or rash or tummy bug is terrifying, and so trips to the doctor are common for these things, as well as the routine check-ups and vaccinations. When you watch 2-year-olds using all the implements in the doctor's kit, you realise just how observant they are and how much they are taking in when at the doctor's surgery. These two aspects of play often overlap, with the 'babies' being subject to many examinations and treatments. However, as seen in a previous photo, they often use their peers as 'patients' too.

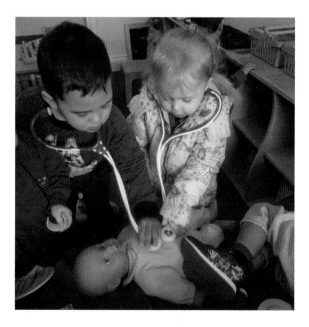

The third role play that has emerged strongly this month has been hairdressing, with several children having had their first real haircut and then talking about this in preschool.

Some children knew that their mum got a 'card' when they left the hairdressers, and this was a perfect opportunity to introduce some mark-making.

Bird watching

Another major interest this month has been the birds that appear in the area just beyond the garden fence. Some of the children began to notice that two birds, in particular, returned over and over again. One was a pigeon and one was a crow. The staff helped the children discover what type of birds they were, and then the children named them Colin the crow and Jeff the wood pigeon. The children then wanted to feed the birds. This led onto discussions and research about what birds would like to eat. The iPads are the perfect resource for this sort of research as they can be used outdoors to identify the birds and then to find out how, and whether, to feed them. The children were keen to make bird feeders, and the staff were keen to involve the parents in this too. Some of the families at the preschool are Muslim, and the parents were not happy for their children to be using pork products such as 'lard' that was one of the ingredients for the hanging bird feeders. However, the parents sent in alternatives such as bird seed, and their children were delighted to be able to contribute to the buzz of excitement.

Block play develops both indoors and outside

Two years ago when the resources were first reduced quite dramatically at the preschool, the staff did worry that the children might not have 'enough' to play with. This month the block play was particularly noticeable, and it is this sort of creative, unique thinking that takes place when the 'one-use wonders' have been removed. So, for example, without a garage for the cars, the children now have to make their own, and without a pre-printed roadway, the children create one themselves. These photos (and the previous one) show just a few of the creations from this month – both indoors and outside. They also show how the children combine resources as they play.

Mark-making

In England at this time, there is incredible pressure from the government and Ofsted to start more formal learning of things like phonics and writing at an ever-earlier age. Their belief is that pushing these things 'earlier' will lead to better results later. This has never been shown to be the case, and, indeed, in my vast experience over four decades, I know that the reverse is true. If we push children to hold a pencil before they are physically ready, they will be put off holding a pencil for a long time. Similarly, if we try to push phonics too soon, again the children will fear this. I would also question – "Why the rush?" I have taught children of all ages, and I know that the easiest age at which to teach phonics is in year one. When they are developmentally ready, you can teach this easily in a matter of a couple of months. We do not need to be forcing these things in preschools. What is also noticeable is that in settings where there is never any pressure to pick up a pencil, the children who are developmentally ready will be seen mark-making very often. They are drawing and writing for all sorts of reasons of their own, in all sorts of formats, with different implements and on different surfaces. It is just another aspect of their play – nothing to be worried about, as there is no pressure to do it. The pictures here show just a few examples that were seen this month, and the 'writing' of appointment cards in the hairdresser's can be seen earlier in this chapter too.

Cousins

As mentioned, children at this young age often play alongside each other rather than with each other. But this does change as they get older, and it is also noticeable how some children appear to form close relationships and definitely do play together. The following photos were taken over just a few days and show how these two children (who are in fact cousins) do have a strong friendship, and it benefits them both. It has also led them to explore new areas of the setting as they each gain confidence from the presence of the other.

'Wow!' moments

I just want to finish this chapter with a couple of 'Wow!' moments. These are events that occurred and made us go 'Wow!' That is why they are note-worthy. This has been mentioned before, but in some settings, the staff try to photograph and document almost everything that occurs, but there is really no point. The examples shown here are something special, out of the ordinary and therefore worth recording.

These flowers were created so simply and yet so effectively, with felt pen marks for the stems and cake papers for the flower heads.

   Here Eymen has sorted a selection of cars by colour and arranged them in lines. It is moments like this which make us realise how competent these very young children are. It also makes us realise how unnecessary it is to set up challenges or tasks – the children will challenge themselves, given the resources, the time, the space and the emotional security to take risks and try things out. Eymen, like all children, is a superb learner. He did not need to be 'taught' how to 'sort by colour' – he needed to be given the resources, time, space and security to allow his innate drive to learn to flourish. Further observation would reveal whether he is in fact also ordering them by the amount of each colour – so the single black car is at one end and the large group of red cars is at the other – 'Wow!' At every moment there are 'Wow!' moments happening in the preschool. The staff realise, however, that the moment is more important than the recording or evidencing of that moment. These moments do demonstrate that the children are making leaps in their development, and January has shown that this is continuing, in spite of the staff being very stretched as they settle new children while continuing to support all the other children as well. As January comes to an end, they are hoping that February will be less stressful but with just as many 'Wow!' moments.

11 February diary

Reading everywhere

When visiting the preschool this month, what struck me was the amount of 'reading' that was happening. These very young children have a love of books and are also beginning to understand that they can be 'useful' too! In this photo, we see Kerry with a group of children, and their deep involvement is obvious to see. These children have not been told to come and listen to the story. One child brought the book over, but once the reading began, children who were nearby and interested were able to shuffle over and join in. With this age group, this is far more powerful, in terms of developing a love of reading, than a structured, lengthy story session at the end of the morning or the end of the day. If books are only read at the end of the day, the children are often too tired or hungry or just want to go home, and the experience is not as positive as it could be. Earlier in the day, they are more 'open' to experiences such as this, because they are not tired, not hungry and not wanting to go home.

The next photo shows one child absorbed in a book, independently of an adult. There are other things worthy of note in this photo, things which, at a glance, could be taken for granted. Firstly, this child has been given the time, space, freedom and environment that has allowed this moment to come about. She was able to go outside when she chose and has already spent a considerable amount of time outside, getting her waterproof clothing on, setting up her resources (in this case a crate and some cushions). She also knew where the books were and chose to select a book and to sit in the crate to 'read' it. However, in addition, the reader should look in the background of the picture to see how other children are deeply engaged in their own chosen pursuits and that an adult is positioned so that they can help an individual child whilst scanning the whole garden area too. Recognise also that the environment has been organised by the adults but that the children have 'ownership' of it and are familiar with it because it does not change. Thus, the waterproof clothing is accessible, has been dried and is ready for the children to access. Similarly, the 'loose parts' – the crates, cushions etc. – are also available and ready to be used as the children decide. The water tray in the background has been filled and the resources stored nearby. This attention to the environment and resources has not happened on this day. It has been like this every day as a result of the hard work of the staff. But the children now know and trust that the environment will be like this every day, and therefore their thought and energy can be put into deciding what to do rather than trying to figure out what is available.

Similarly, indoors, the children know where the books are kept (in various locations indoors) and they can select them to read whenever they wish. They also know that if they want an adult to read to them, then the adults are usually free to do this – they are not sat at tables doing 'focus tasks' – their job is to observe the children and to interact whenever and wherever they can. In the next photos, we see children who have opted to read independently of the adults and on their own.

The next photo shows how **young children learn from each other**, and this is another theme that has been more apparent in the recent months. Although children aged 24 months do not play as 'socially' as 4-year-olds, they do enjoy the company of other children, and they learn by observing and 'imitating' others. Thus, when one child opts to sit and read at a table, then others might do this too.

In the photo that follows, we see a child accessing a 'non-fiction' book in a way that is relevant and meaningful to such young children. Betsy remembered how they identified the birds from this book, and when the birds reappeared she was able to find the book and point out the pictures of the birds within the book. This sort of 'first-hand' experience is so powerful in terms of learning. We can tell children about 'non-fiction' books, or we can use them in the way they are meant to be used. It is obvious which approach will have most impact on learning – 3D active learning – using the book and looking at real birds, as opposed to 2D passive learning – just reading the book indoors without the real birds.

Versatile resources and versatile staff

In the next series of photos, we see the power of open-ended, versatile resources as well as the importance of having staff who are flexible and 'open' in their approach. Staff need to be willing and able to adapt as situations arise. Rather than seeing unexpected events as a problem, try to view them as an opportunity. So a very windy day will lead to new learning, as will a snowy day, a foggy day, a leaking roof, some spilt paint, a broken toy, a worm, a rainbow, a puddle etc. If staff are not willing to respond to unexpected or unplanned events, then a setting can become very stressful but also quite 'dull'. Indeed, that is another problem in settings where everything is pre-planned, because the staff are almost 'resentful' when something unexpected occurs which could disrupt their 'plans'. In such situations, they often ignore the snow or the birds or the worm or the BOX because **it is not on the planning!** When working 'in the moment', such unexpected events are welcomed, embraced and enjoyed. Thus, when a delivery was made to the building, the box was brought into the garden and the learning began. At the end of the day, the box was brought indoors, and the next day, the learning took a new direction with mark-making on numerous planes.

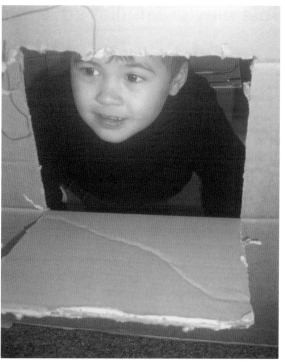

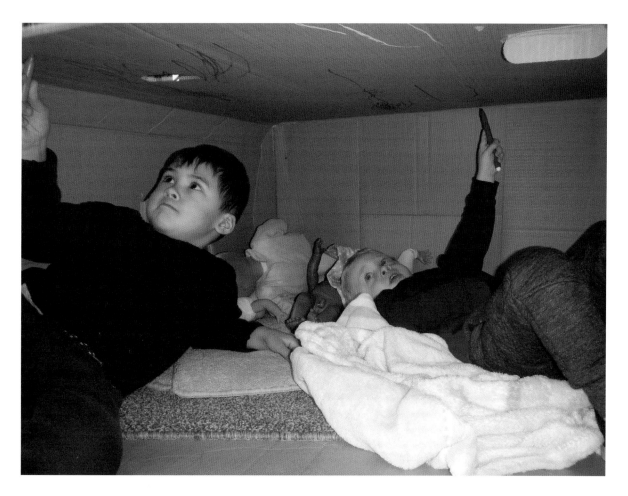

Role play of familiar situations continues

As mentioned previously, young children learn by imitation, and the role-play that was so evident in January has continued into this month and will pervade the play of children for years to come. Again, the domestic role play dominates, and a child-sized apron will appeal as it so closely resembles something a parent might wear. In the photo on the right, we can see the hairdressing resources in the background, but these have now lost their appeal somewhat and the recurrent play of 'shopping' is surfacing. Again, the adaptability of the resources, the staff and the space is key if the true interests of the children are to emerge. If the staff were insistent on the hairdressing carrying on for a set amount of time, then the play would have become low-level and not purposeful, whereas, if the children are leading the play, then as their interest changes, the environment and the staff adapt to maintain the deeper involvement and to therefore maximise the learning.

Children learn from each other

The 'peer to peer' learning has been evident in all the examples given above – the reading, the BOX, the role play and one final example is shown in the next two photos. One child is seen observing her peer succeeding in traversing the 'tipping bridge' and this is enough motivation to prompt the attempt and eventual success for herself. These children learnt without an adult in this moment, but the work of the adults is implicit in this event. They have set up the environment with the appropriate resourcing, but crucially, they have given the children the confidence, the social skills and the resilience that they need for this sort of learning. The role of the adult in this moment was to stand back and allow the children to take their learning forward themselves.

Expanding horizons

I am often asked by practitioners about how children will be exposed to new experiences if we don't 'plan' them in advance or if we don't offer them new experiences at all. My response reflects back to the levels of involvement – if the children are displaying **deep levels of involvement** for as much time as possible, then we know their brains are developing, we **know they are making progress** and we know that they will be able to take on new learning as they get older.

We also know that for this deep involvement to be displayed, their well-being is high too. Without good well-being – including confidence, resilience, a feeling of security – they will not be able to become deeply involved – that is, to take on new learning. With this as the priority and vision – 'to have happy and engaged children' – we do not need to worry about the 'content' of their experiences, rather the type of experiences. When a child is playing with blocks, or mud or fabric; when they are climbing or cutting or peeling a satsuma; when they are asking questions or chatting to a worm or listening to a story – it is their level of involvement that indicates whether the experience is valuable or not.

We also know that children become most deeply involved when they have chosen the activity rather than when it is an activity chosen by an adult. The learning in self-chosen activity is more likely and more easily hard-wired and retained. As adults, we know this from our own experiences of life and learning. For example, I do not know the rules of football because I have never been interested in playing football or watching football. However, I know a lot about horses because I am interested and engaged by them. So when thinking about offering new experiences to young children, consider if the effort is worthwhile. Consider whether the children are really interested or not. Consider if the experience will have any long-term impact on their development.

Festivals and celebrations are often the subject of these discussions, and there are several events almost every month in England – harvest festival, Halloween, firework night, Remembrance Sunday, Christmas, New Year, Mother's day, Father's day, Easter, and so on. If we add in the events from other religions–Eid, Chinese New Year, Yom Kippur, Diwali and so on, it is easy to see how we could be trying to introduce one such event almost every week in a setting.

We need to consider if this is worthwhile in terms of the learning and development of such young children. What do we value, and what values do we want the children to develop? Most major belief systems have a similar 'core', and it is up to each setting to develop their own 'mini-culture' with its own 'core beliefs'. So, for example, a team might agree that they want the children to be kind, friendly, cooperative, helpful and so on. But there is no need to set up particular experiences to develop these characteristics – they will pervade every moment of the practice in the setting. So the staff will talk to the children about how there are not many strawberries, and so they should only eat one each to ensure that everyone can have one. They will remind the children to tidy up their room so that other children can enjoy the space. They will ensure that a child looks at and helps take care of a child who has been hurt. In this way, the 'culture' of the setting is defined and developed, and there is no need to cover numerous festivals and events from the calendar, which are often meaningless and not appropriate for such young children.

A few children will celebrate Eid in their homes, and they might talk about this in preschool, but it is not necessary for the other children to learn the 'facts' about Eid. The important aspect of development here is that they are learning that each child and each family is different: "Other families do things in their way and it is different to the way my family do things." They will also learn from this that this is how life is and that these differences are interesting and fine – just another aspect of life. Even two Muslim children will learn that their lives are different – one might live with both parents, one might live just with their mum. "Culture" is defined as "the ideas, customs, and social behaviours of a particular people or society" – and that will be different for each and every child.

Chinese New Year occurred in February in 2019 and one of the children started talking about the dragon they saw on TV. When a staff member mentioned Chinese New Year, another child said, "We have Chinese noodles from the take-away." The interest emerged and the staff observed and responded, leading to a trip to the shops, cooking noodles and eating them at the snack table. In many settings, this would have been a pre-planned activity, and the staff would be thinking about the learning related to 'other cultures and celebrations' etc. However, for children aged 2 and 3, the learning is not about that at all. The images of the dragon on TV had obviously had an impact on one child, and this led on to other things. In terms of learning from these events, the children developed in all areas of learning, but I do not think that any one of them will be able to tell you about Chinese New Year if we asked them the next week. They will remember the trip to the shops and eating the noodles, just as they remember playing in the BIG BOX, building with the blocks, walking on the wobbly bridge and so on. They remember the things that interest them – the 'facts' around Chinese New Year are irrelevant to most of their lives and therefore will not be retained. However, they will remember what it was like to try new food, how that felt a bit 'scary' for some, but how it was a 'good' experience overall and therefore something they will be willing to try again in future. Thus, they have built a bit more resilience – another block in their stock of positive experiences which help them go on to be willing to try other new experiences.

New experiences can be the simplest things too

My other response to questions about 'broadening horizons' is that most of what is on offer in a preschool or nursery is a new experience for a child. Indeed, just being in a group setting is a new experience, being away from a parent, being with other children for long periods, having to learn new 'rules and expectations' and having access to new resources are all new experiences which 'broaden the horizons' from a home life. We need to keep things simple and not 'over-think' the role of a preschool. Reflect on and value every experience in the day – no matter how small. So putting on boots, digging in the sand, looking at a book, building with the blocks – these are all experiences which broaden horizons.

With this in mind – look at the next series of photos and reflect on the learning that is taking place, look at the levels of involvement of the children, consider what the role of the adults has been in order for these events to come about and remember that this deep involvement means that the child is learning and developing in this moment – new learning is happening and resilience is growing – and that learning and resilience will allow the child to develop further at the next moment, the next hour, the next day, the next week or the next year. It is this 'capacity to learn' that should be our main priority to nurture in preschool, not the coverage of facts or festivals that may or may not be of interest to a child.

12 March diary

Surprising warm, dry weather

The weather in March 2019 was surprisingly warm and dry, which meant that many children opted to be outdoors for even longer than usual. Even though the resources in the garden have not changed, the children continue to find new ways to use them. Sometimes this happens completely independently and sometimes with a prompt from an adult. Thus, in this photo, we see how a shopping basket is being used as a resource through which the pipes can be fed and held – allowing the children to explore the flow of water without having to hold the pipes in place. This is something that the children have seen indoors before, but they are now able to transfer this knowledge and to organise this themselves outdoors.

Adult 'teaching' leads to independence later

Every time I visit the preschool, I see examples of adults directing or guiding the play, and I also see examples of children doing things independently that, on previous visits, were being guided. This is the essence of quality early years practice. The staff trust the children to indicate their interests – through the choices that they make. They observe carefully and decide whether or not to get involved with the play. If they do decide to interact, they try not to 'hijack' the play to their own agenda but rather to add sensitively so that the interest and involvement of the children is maintained but also so that they 'add' to the play in some way. If their interaction is skilful, their teaching will be at just the right level for the particular child in that particular moment, meaning that the child is able to take the new learning on. It is at exactly the right level of challenge for that particular child. In addition, in the hours, days or weeks that follow, the children will apply this new learning independently, thus consolidating this next step and, at the same time, continuing to build their resilience, independence and confidence.

For example, during one visit, I observed the following interaction:

Observation: Kayla was struggling to sit the Duplo person in the car.
Teaching: 'T' explained that the arms were in the way and suggested that Kayla push them up.
Outcome: Kayla pushed the arms up and then sat the person in the car.

Independent learning

The next time I was at the preschool, Kayla had a row of cars, each with a person sat in them – all with their arms pushed up.

This seems such a simple interaction and yet there are many less positive ways in which this could have developed:

● If the adults had been involved in focus activities, they might not have noticed that Kayla was trying to do this, and she might have abandoned the task completely.
● An adult who was less skilled might have taken the Duplo character, pushed the arms up and sat it in the car. In this case Kayla would not

have learnt the skill for herself and next time would have faced the same frustration.

- If the setting was organised so that resources are rotated each day or each week, then the Duplo might not have been available on another day for Kayla to consolidate her learning at a later date.
- In some settings, the adults leave the children to struggle with things, believing that this is how they learn best. In some situations this is absolutely the case. However, the skilful adult will know just when to step in. In this case, it was clear that Kayla was not going to figure this out for herself, and the adult made the right decision and did not stand back for too long.
- Another possibility is that the adult might have got involved but then diverted the learning onto something that was on the adult agenda – such as colours or numbers etc. In this case, there is a possibility that Kayla might have learnt something, but the opportunity to learn the particular skill that she was interested in at that moment would have been lost.

This is a simple, yet powerful, example of child-initiated play and how the role of the adult is critical within this – to observe carefully, to reflect on the particular child and to 'plan in the moment' as to how to respond. They will then interact to guide and/or direct the play – modelling language, demonstrating skills, explaining, facilitating, encouraging, etc. With each tiny success that a child experiences, particularly if it has involved an appropriate level of challenge, then their resilience will increase. They are then in a better position emotionally to face the next challenge. Once this resilience is strong, we see children tackling new learning independently, confident in the knowledge that an adult will be there to support them if they need it. We then see children learning and developing independently. At this point in the year, this is absolutely evident in the children in the preschool.

Learning by playing in a group

The next series of photos show exactly this. Without an adult, the children explore and experiment, supporting each other at times and then working independently at other times. In each photo, reflect on the fact that the role of the adult is implicit. The adults have organised the environment and the resources, they have established a routine which gives the children long periods of time and they have established the expectations about behavior so that each child feels safe. But they have also developed in the children their independence, their confidence and their resilience, resulting in children who are able to spend long periods experimenting, exploring and learning. You will also see that the adults are still present and in some instances will interact and then step back. They offer enough support but not too much – a simple thing to say and a hugely complex thing to do in practice.

In the preceding picture, we see Poppy watching another child and, in the following picture, experimenting with this herself.

In these next few photos, we see a few children experimenting together. They realise through their play that, when the end of the pipe is down, that the water flows out; if the end of the pipe is higher, the water does not flow; and finally, with great cooperation, they can adjust the level and position of the pipe to get the water to flow into a container.

In the next photo, we see Poppy again. She has made a scientific discovery that water can bounce! Who knows how this new-found knowledge will be applied?

Children stay involved if the suggestions are appropriate

Young children are drawn to balls and will use them in their play in numerous different ways. On one occasion in March, Hayley noticed a large group who were gathering up various balls, and she decided to introduce them to the activity of bouncing the balls on fabric. While doing this, she was observing the children, and if their level of involvement had not been high, she would have abandoned the activity. However, it is clear from their body language and their faces that the activity was appealing, challenging and fun. This is something that they will repeat on other days, with or without an adult. This is another example of 'expanding horizons' as discussed in the February chapter (Chapter 11). If adults are observant and creative, they will 'think on their feet' and introduce things at exactly the right moment to exploit a current interest. If the children were too young, or if they had done this too many times before, or if they were trying to organise a game of football, or in many other instances, the interaction would not have been successful and the children would not have engaged. However, in this instance, the appropriateness of the interaction and the suggestion is clear to see.

Water play is just as engaging indoors

Indoors, the fascination with water is also evident, as it is every day with children of this age. Some of the resources in the water area indoors had been damaged and scratched – just through the usual wear and tear in a busy room. With refreshed resources, the children can now see the water within the containers again, leading to new discussions and discoveries.

Making a feast

The next few photos show a few children playing together to create a feast. The level of involvement is so high that they don't even notice the camera or the adult who is holding it. This is a superb example of children developing and learning from each other, cooperating, discussing, planning and compromising. However, this does not happen without the interactions from adults that have been occurring all year. The children have been taught how to talk to each other, how to 'negotiate' and how to empathise. Thus, by this point in the year, this level of independent play is possible.

Decisions about Mother's Day and Red Nose Day

Mother's Day and Red Nose Day occurred in March in 2019, and these are two events that I am often asked about. As discussed in the February chapter, it is important to reflect on how meaningful these events are for 2-year-olds and what aspect, if any, of the traditions surrounding these events will be meaningful and relevant to children of this age. Also, consider whether the benefits of doing something around such events is worth the disruption it will cause. So for Mother's Day, some children will enjoy making a card, but others won't. Some children will be living with their mum and others won't. Some staff will feel very strongly that the children should make a card. As a team, this needs to be discussed. At Staple Hill, the decision was made to leave some card and resources in the creative area and to give the children the opportunity to make a card if they wished. If any child did not make a card, then the staff explained to the parent that they would not force a child to do the activity. Many children did produce cards and each was unique – another important factor if such activities are going to occur.

  With regard to Red Nose Day, for very young children, the appealing feature of this event is the red nose itself. I do not believe that children of this age should be thinking about world poverty or starvation. They should be protected from such distressing things in their earliest years. However, a red nose is fun, the children will have seen them everywhere and it will inevitably be mentioned in the preschool. At Staple Hill, there was very little fuss – red noses were dabbed onto any child who wanted one and the play continued.

Supporting physical development

Physical development – gross and fine motor control – is often a cause for concern amongst practitioners. My response is always that, given the right environment, resources and opportunities, there is no need for any sort of 'intervention' at this stage in education. The provision *is* the intervention. If a child were in a home where the TV was on all day and they rarely had any opportunities to move around, handle tools, climb etc., then physical development might be delayed. However, in a setting, this should not be the case. With access to outdoors all day and appropriate resourcing indoors and outdoors, the children will challenge themselves and their physical development will flourish. The next few photos show children engaging in physical activity of various sorts. All these pursuits were chosen by the children, and the variety and range is obvious. Both gross and fine motor control are being developed in numerous areas of the room and garden. These photos should also make practitioners reflect on the absurdity of trying to segment the curriculum. Children are physical in everything that they do, they are communicating continuously, they are being social whenever they are near another child.

One of the major events that occurred in April was that the woodwork bench was introduced. The bench has been at the setting for a few weeks, but the staff were waiting for all the new children to be settled so that they could afford to allocate one adult to the woodwork area during the period when it was being introduced. The staff have not had woodwork for this age group before, and they understandably feel nervous. We have discussed the benefits as well as the potential risks, and the staff have decided that they will only open the bench when they can have an adult there for 1–1 support to begin with. They have positioned the bench so that other children can watch but cannot get too close to the moving hammer.

If we could scan the brain of the child in the photo at the beginning of this chapter, we would see great activity – powerful learning and rapid progress. Such deep-level involvement is always found at the woodwork benches. We must keep this in mind with all activities and resources that we are offering. Why are we offering them? What are the benefits? What learning will they bring? Of course, we must consider the risks, but 'Risk

Assessments', by their nature, focus on the negative aspects of an activity. I always prefer to write a 'Benefit/Risk Assessment'. In this way, you focus on why you are doing a particular activity before thinking about the possible risks and how to mitigate them. The assessment here demonstrates clearly that the benefits of woodwork far outweigh the risks.

Benefits

Woodwork is the perfect activity in which children can demonstrate the characteristics of effective learning:

- **Playing and exploring** – children investigate and experience things, and 'have a go'.
- **Active learning** – children concentrate and keep on trying if they encounter difficulties, and enjoy achievements.
- **Creating and thinking critically** – children have and develop their own ideas, make links between ideas, and develop strategies for doing things.

Also all the seven areas of learning in the current EYFS framework will be developed:-

Physical development: With the use of real tools and hard wood (rather than balsa wood), the muscles in the hands and arms become stronger and the children develop more control of these muscles. They learn to vary the amount of force used – with hammers and saws. They also develop hand-eye coordination in order to hit the nails. Fine motor control is developed as children hold the thin nails in place. Through experience they learn how to keep their fingers out of the way of the hammer.

Personal, social and emotional development: children demonstrate deep levels of involvement when undertaking a woodwork task. Often, children who normally will not persevere at a task are prepared to try for far longer at woodwork – perhaps because they realise it is something truly challenging but also 'real'. Children will return to unfinished work the following day if necessary. They learn to share and take turns, negotiating and discussing routines and rules. They learn how to keep themselves and others safe. They realise that a real hammer can do serious harm, and they do treat the tools with respect. They learn to follow agreed rules. Children who find it difficult to conform are often so keen to participate that they do manage to comply with requests and boundaries at the woodwork bench – just so that they get their turn. They take great pride in their achievements, and therefore their self-esteem is boosted. For most children woodwork is a new activity, and therefore they are taking a risk just by becoming involved – they take further risks using the equipment but learn to do this safely and independently. As with all experiences, this type of 'struggle' resulting in 'success', no matter how small, will increase their stock of resilience.

Communication and language development: There is always a lot of discussion at the workbench, and therefore language is developed. Children have to follow instructions and will often be heard explaining the rules to other children. They encounter problems all the time and discuss solutions. They explain what they are doing and learn the vocabulary associated with the activity.

Creative development: With many activities for young children, the process is as important (if not more important) than the product. This is definitely the case when children are first starting at woodwork. They need to develop the techniques. Eventually, they will start to use their imagination, combined with their knowledge of the task, to plan what to make. With support, they will have learnt how it is possible to combine various materials and media, and this will increase their options and possibilities.

Knowledge of the world: Clearly, through working with wood, the children will learn about its properties and the properties of other materials that they combine with the wood. They will learn about how to use tools and how to combine different materials. With appropriate interactions, they could learn about the source of wood and various types of wood. They will be experiencing the process of 'design, make, review'.

Mathematical development: This pervades every aspect of the task – from experiencing the weight and size of the wood to deciding how many wheels to add to a truck. Children will be thinking about size and shape as well as number. Again, with appropriate interaction, their thoughts can be vocalised, refined and developed.

Literacy development: Children will often combine mark-making with woodwork – adding drawn features to their models. They also add their name to ensure their work is not lost. They will use books to refer to for ideas or information.

There are not many activities which appeal to so many children and have such broad and deep learning potential.

Risks and actions

Hazard	Possible scale of injury	Precautions to put in place to reduce risk	Risk rating
General risk of injury through use and misuse of tools	Medium	Staff will ensure that children are closely supervised during the induction period until all children have been trained in the use of the tools and comply with the "Two children at each bench" rule. Staff will then remain vigilant in watching the woodwork area. Adults all aware of how to get first aid help if necessary.	Low

Hazard	Possible scale of injury	Precautions to put in place to reduce risk	Risk rating
Children with behavioural difficulties/ developmental delay might not adhere to the rules and might not use the tools safely	Medium	Staff will ensure close supervision of these children if they are near the woodwork area.	Low
Sawdust in eyes	Low	Children to wear goggles on windy days.	Low
Hit fingers with hammer	Low	Train children to tap lightly to fix nail in place and then move hand away when they hit harder.	Low
Children get hit by moving tools	Medium	Strict imposition of two children only limit at the bench. Staff will be scanning and monitoring the area at all times.	Low
Cut with saw	Low	Strict rule – 'wood in vice'.	Low
Splinters	Low	Wood will be checked. Children shown how to use sandpaper.	Low
Sharp nails cause injury	Low	Protruding nails will be hammered down. Children will not remove nails from work area.	Low

Clearly the benefits are great and the risks can be managed.

(It should be noted that where woodwork has been introduced, I do not know of any serious accidents at the woodwork benches, and even minor incidents are rare.)

Practicalities

Induction and access: The benches should be outdoors (the noise would be unbearable indoors) and in an area that can be seen at all times. At Staple Hill, the bench was introduced mid-year, but it is preferable for it to be available when the children first start and with an adult beside the bench at all times to begin with. Staff could encourage parents to help ensure that the children adhere to the very simple rules: two children at each bench, two hands on the saw. There must be a zero tolerance of any dangerous behaviour, and the children quickly learn to behave appropriately if they want to be involved. The woodwork should be part of the continuous, outstanding provision – always available and, therefore, it will not cause a 'mad rush' of children trying to have a turn. After the induction period, adults should 'keep an eye' on the woodwork area, but an adult does not always need to be 'stationed' there. At Staple Hill, the staff team have decided that they will open the bench regularly but will have an adult present all the time. Each staff team must make these decisions themselves. They are the people who know the children best and can therefore make these decisions.

Equipment: I would recommend "stubby" hammers, smooth fine nails (bought by the kilo from an ironmonger) and adult-size hack-saws. At Staple Hill, in the 2–3 garden, the staff have just introduced hammers and not the saws. These will be introduced when the children move to the larger garden with the older children. The workbench from 'Creative Cascade UK Ltd' is sturdy and a very reasonable price. www.creativecascade.co.uk/products/wood-works/

Additional resources: You can add a variety of resources for children to fix to the wood such as milk bottle tops, elastic bands, fabric, Corex, corks, buttons, string etc. Paint, felt pens and pencils should be available to decorate models as well.

Wood: Wood is too expensive to buy. The best option is to find a local timber merchant who offers a 'cutting service' for customers. They are usually happy to keep off-cuts for use by children – you can take a large bin to the timber yard which they fill up with off-cuts, and you can then collect the wood every few weeks.

Woodwork leads to deep learning and outstanding progress in all areas of development. Children are attracted to the challenges it brings and fascinated by the possibilities. Adults can be anxious about this activity, but I would urge settings to have a go – the resulting engagement and learning will amaze and delight adults and children alike.

Mini-beasts

Staple Hill Stars Pre-school is in a city, adjacent to a car park with very little 'green space' or trees etc. However, even within their small garden, the staff have ensured that there are places to attract mini-beasts – a few potted plants, some muddy banks around the edge of the garden, the sand etc. The discovery of mini-beasts within the garden has sparked this interest amongst several children during this month, and so the staff made several trips beyond the garden fence to the small weedy bank near the entrance, which is the perfect habitat for mini-beasts.

This snail was reluctant to leave the cup to transfer to the pan, but Asude showed perseverance and calm as she waited for the snail to complete the journey.

The calm and focus is palpable in this picture too – for such a young child to have a butterfly on their hand is remarkable.

Resources reviewed

The staff at the preschool continue to review the resources and reflect on the levels of involvement that they deliver. Early in their journey, the staff agreed to let go of numerous resources but decided to keep others. We had discussions about the dolls' house, the car park and the dressing up clothes, but the staff team were reluctant to let these go. However, in recent weeks, they have seen that the children are not using the dolls' house or the car park – they are creating their own! So, these resources have now been removed from the room. The next two photos show two of the houses that have been created in recent weeks. In the photo on the left, the dolls' house can be seen (not in use) in the background. When looking at these structures, consider the amount of brain activity and learning that was required to create them, as opposed to the brain activity needed to use a ready-made dolls' house.

In a similar development, the staff have discussed the dressing up clothes and have decided to replace these with pieces of fabric and pegs etc. Again, this has been a long process of discussion, observation and reflection. The staff are aware that the children enjoy wearing the princess dresses (as seen in the next photo), but they are also aware of the arguments that these costumes cause and also the limited learning that they bring. Without the ready-made costumes, the children now make their own – again resulting in increased brain activity and learning.

Visuals

As mentioned earlier in the book, Makaton is used with all the children in the preschool. For some children, visual cues on cards are helpful as well, and several children have recently become interested in these. They have been asking to wear the cards around their necks like the staff. This was a perfect opportunity to suggest that the children could make their own, and with some support and some scribing, the children made their own collections of cards.

For a term-time setting, April was a very short month in 2019. However, the children had some very memorable experiences in these weeks, with the events described in this chapter being just a tiny sample of these.

14 | May diary

During the month of May, some of the children in the 2–3 room demonstrated a leap in their development in terms of their increased awareness of their environment (both within and beyond the preschool) and also in their awareness of differences and similarities to other children. This development resulted in requests for particular activities which the children had experienced before, such as cooking and trips beyond the immediate environment. It also led to discussions between children about their families as well as opportunities to help the children develop negotiation skills – putting their increased awareness and vocabulary to good use.

Cooking

Every time there are opportunities to cook, we see deep involvement and enjoyment in the children. Whilst the youngest children join in with any and all events, some of the older children now request things that they remember from earlier occasions. Thus when the play dough runs out, there are several children who know that this is an opportunity for some 'cooking', and whenever possible, the staff respond and support this request, as shown in this photo.

Watermelon

When the fruit at the snack table was running low, one of the children mentioned their love of watermelon and requested to go and buy some for the children. This resulted in great excitement and discussions as the need for some money was explored and a visit to the office took place. Once some money was secured, the trip to the local shop was a great success, as the watermelon was available. Returning to the preschool to share the fruit with the other children led to further learning and consideration of the needs of all the children.

Awareness of other children

Sharing the melon was one example of the increasing awareness of other children that is evident in the group. Other examples were seen when the children were looking at their special books. The younger children are keen to look at their own book, whereas the older children wanted to look at their friends' books and to talk about the images and items that they saw.

This increased awareness amongst the children means that the staff can continue to work on the children's negotiation skills. Whenever there is a dispute, they try to give the children the language and strategies to use to sort the dispute out themselves. With the improved language and awareness, this is proving even more successful. Thus, the children can say "Can I have a turn now?" or "Stop that! I don't like it" – simple but powerful phrases that children can learn and use in future situations.

Another event occurred which led to a further development of awareness about differences amongst families; a new baby visited the setting. From this simple event, the children will be realizing that some children have younger siblings and others don't. This is just the sort of experience that is relevant to children of this age and is an appropriate way of exploring differences and similarities. A child who has no siblings will realise that other children do have siblings. The important thing is that the differences are apparent but that one situation is respected as much as any other. This is the ultimate in 'tolerance' at this age. The children do not need to learn about the facts of Islam, Christianity or other family traditions. They simply need to begin to understand that everyone is slightly different and that this is fine.

New trolleys!

Throughout the year, the staff review and reflect on the resources in the preschool, and if there is any extra money then decisions are made very carefully about how this should be spent. Over the course of the year, several doll's buggies have been broken, and so too have some wheelbarrows. The team decided to purchase two trolleys from Community Playthings and, although quite expensive, they are hopeful that the high quality and strength of these resources will mean that they last a long time. In addition, the versatility has been immediately evident, as the children use them as cars, for transporting resources, as push-chairs and as wheelchairs.

Cars

Some interests persist, and 'cars' is one such passion. The toy cars are always popular; children often build vehicles with the blocks, they wash the vehicles, spot cars in the adjacent car park and request to see real cars. As with all such requests, if the staff can facilitate this, then they do.

The final picture in this chapter shows a group of children who have managed to play alongside each other, working together to build a complex structure. This is quite remarkable in a room that is for 2- to 3-year-olds.

For an event such as this to come about is the culmination of months of 'teaching' by the staff team. The staff have ensured that:

- The environment is organised to ensure that structures like this are in an area that is 'protected' – there is a 'barrier' around the area so that other children do not run across the carpet and knock into things that are being created.
- The resources available are a mixture of open-ended materials combined with things that the children play purposefully with but cannot make for themselves (such as animals, figures, cars etc.).
- The children are aware of the expectations – so they do not break models that other children have made (understanding that this will upset another child); they do not run and shout in this area (understanding that if they want to run and shout, they can go outside to do this); they listen to the ideas of other children (beginning to realise that, as a group, they can create something possibly more interesting than they could do on their own).
- The children can express their feelings, and children empathise with each other. This means that they can express their frustration if another child

takes a resource that they are using, and they will respond if another child is upset or angry.

● The physical development of the children has been supported through numerous opportunities, both indoors and outside – meaning that they can now move around in this small space, manipulating objects without knocking into each other or knocking the structure down.

Remarkable in so many ways!

Review and reflect on the year

June is often a month when **staff review the year** and reflect on any areas that need developing or changing. This includes the environment, resources, routines but also expectations etc. This year, one of the discussions was around the 'rules' for the 2–3 provision. It seemed that a few staff members were not absolutely clear about the rules, and if the adults are inconsistent, then this quickly translates into behavior issues amongst the children. Thus, the team spent a staff meeting going over the rules in the hope that with the new intake, the consistency would be ensured from day one. In June there were also lots of visits from new children and their families, and so it was critical that these rules were established and consistent for these visitors too.

The preschool do actually have very few rules, but they are as follows:

- Inside we walk
- Inside we use quiet voices
- When we have finished playing, we put things away
- Indoor toys stay indoors
- We do climbing outside

(They do also insist on the children wearing aprons when playing with the water and waterproofs when it is raining outside.)

Rolling lunch

In discussions and reflections, the staff were concerned that the level of involvement at lunchtimes was often very low. Also, the routines around lunch were causing some children distress and causing the staff a certain degree of stress. The routine was complicated, as some children arrive at 12, others leave at 12 and others stay all day. The routine was that just before 12, all children were stopped and the whole environment was tidied. All children were then gathered so that the tables could be cleared and arranged for lunch, some children went home with their parents and the others were ushered into the toilets for hand-washing. The children who arrived at 12 also had to go straight to wash their hands ready for lunch. Thus, there was anxiety for the children who were being confined to the back room and to washing their hands. There was also great anxiety for children who just arrived at 12 and who had to go straight to wash their hands and then sit down for lunch. For several children, this was not what they wanted to do when they first arrived. It also meant that the transition and handover from their parents was often distressing because the children were not happy and therefore reluctant to leave their parents.

The staff decided to trial a different system in which there would be a 'rolling lunch' option, in the same way as there is a 'rolling snack' option. The parents were all sent a letter to inform them of the changes, and all parents were supportive of the changes since the rationale was so clear and reasoned.

The lunch system was therefore changed in June, and it has been a totally positive experience. What happens now is that at about 11 am the snack table becomes a lunch table and five or six children at a time can sit and have their lunch. By about 1 pm all children will have eaten. The advantages of this are numerous. The children are not interrupted in their play but rather can be invited to eat when they have a natural gap in their play or when they are hungry. The children who arrive at 12 do not have to immediately go and wash their hands and sit down to lunch. Instead, they can go and play, and this means that their transition and saying goodbye to a parent is much easier because they are involved in play and happy. In addition, the room does not have to be disrupted in terms of the use of space. The tables for play dough and creative activities can continue to be used for these things, as it is just the snack table that is used for lunch. Also, the staff don't have to clean the whole area and reset it after lunch. The social aspect of the meal is maintained and is in fact better with a smaller group and an adult sitting with the group.

At Staple Hill, the children bring their own lunch, but I have seen this system now working in several settings where hot meals are provided for the children. These settings have heat-preserving boxes, and the food stays at the required temperature for about an hour and a half. Therefore, their 'rolling lunch' station can be open for that whole period.

It is a credit to the staff team at Staple Hill that they now prioritise the well-being and involvement of the children to such a degree that they were able to make this change for the benefit of the children.

Transition arrangements continue

June is also the month when **transition** routines continue, and at Staple Hill, one of the things they do is to make a transition booklet for the children that are moving from the toddler room to the preschool room. One of the main things in the booklet is photos of the staff (Shaneen, the room leader, is shown here) as well as photos of various areas of the environment, including the entrance, the toilets and the outside areas. Each child that is moving up to this room was given a copy of the booklet to take home. This means that, through the summer holiday, they could look at the booklet and talk about the photos with a parent/carer. The summer holiday goes very quickly for adults, but for young children it is a long time, and booklets such as this will help keep things in their mind.

Transitions into the toddler room are also high on the agenda during this month. The new children come for visits, and therefore the staff ensure that their key person has already been chosen so that they can begin to build a bond with them. If the new child has had a sibling in the preschool, then the staff would try to have the same key person if there is a good relationship already, as this means that knowledge about the family is already in place. This can support a smoother transition. It is also useful during these early visits to find out if any outside agencies are involved with a family so that any additional support can be applied for if necessary.

For the children leaving the toddler room, the visits to the preschool room are another essential part of the transition process. This year the children were particularly attracted to the more challenging climbing equipment and the wheeled toys, as these photos show.

Another important part of these visits is about spending time with the adults in the room so that the relationship and trust can begin to build.

Toilet training continues

As in most toddler rooms, toilet training is an important aspect of the work. This year has been no different, and as the end of the year approaches, the staff are using parent meetings to really push for this to be prioritised at home as well, especially for children who are moving up to the preschool room. The 1–1 meetings when staff meet to discuss the focus child week (see Chapter 5 for details) is the perfect opportunity to discuss this with individual parents, sharing ideas and strategies that parents could use during the summer break.

A visit from Shelley the tortoise was a memorable event from this month too. Kaz was given a tortoise as a pet and, having checked out all the benefits and potential risks, decided that the children would benefit greatly from meeting this little animal. The group in the toddler room (again as in all toddler rooms) are fascinated by living things – be that the snails in the garden, the birds in the carpark or the dog walking past in the street. The chance to be close to another animal was enticing and led to development in numerous areas.

Discussions began and the children wanted to know what the tortoise would eat. They have spent many hours watching the birds outside and investigating what they would eat, and so this was a logical point of interest. Kaz explained about what she fed the tortoise at home and suggested that the children might be able to find some dandelions for Shelley to eat. After some further discussion about what dandelions were, the children searched, visited the preschool garden and looked along the pavements outside the preschool. Eventually, they found the right plant and enjoyed feeding the tortoise.

Some children decided to draw the tortoise and others made a tortoise out of play dough.

A few children decided they would like to hold the tortoise. This is a perfect example of 'risk taking', when thought of as 'anything new' (as Kathryn Solly describes it in her work). The 'risk' is the 'newness' of the experience and causes new synapse formation as the child sees and touches the shell up close, feels the texture of the feet as the tortoise moves, takes its weight and adjusts their hand to compensate for this. Such 'everyday' things are new to a 2-year-old, and their brain is being pushed to adjust and grow in response. Each new experience causes further brain growth and learning which will be reinforced over and over in similar situations. In addition, because the experience with Shelley was a positive one for these children, their resilience will have been further increased. They had a new, potentially 'worrying' experience and came through it with good feelings and memories. This will hold them in good stead for the next 'new/risky' experience that comes along. This is a life-long gift: resilient children who are ready to take on new challenges.

In July, Staple Hill Stars preschool experienced the extremes of weather, but the beginning of the month was very hot. The temporary sunshades were put up so that the children could continue to access the garden all day. Some of the children commented that it looked like a "party". One child said "We have one of those for the barbeque party." Several children were excited by talk of parties in general, and so the idea took hold and the children started to play parties. A suggestion of decorations also came from one of the children, and the adults made suggestions about this. The children in the chapter's opening photo are making items to thread onto string as 'bunting', and they can be seen using a hole punch to makes holes for the string to go through. A few days later, the parents were invited to stay for some songs and stories under the shelter, and several families joined this event.

Dressing up clothes are one of the resources which the staff have been discussing, and in the last month or so, they have replaced all the ready-made dressing up costumes with pieces of fabric, pegs and string. This means that the children have been making their own costumes. Daisy had obviously been talking about this at home and had insisted on turning an adult's T-shirt into an outfit. She then decided to wear this to preschool and kept it on for the whole session!

Penguins in the sun!

In spite of the heat, the children continue to be as lively as ever, and as long as they are well hydrated, wear sun hats and have plenty of sunscreen, the play in the outdoor area continues all day. In this photo, the group are singing and acting out the Penguin Song. This led to discussions about the snow and the difference to the weather in July. But the singing and 'penguin walking' continued.

Local trips continue

As the year has progressed, the children have become more assertive in their requests for particular activities, and trips to the shops are a frequent suggestion. On one occasion, the children asked to return the fruit tray to the local greengrocer who supplies the fruit and salad items for the snack table. Whilst out to complete this little task, further opportunities were taken advantage of. For example, crossing roads, listening to various vehicles, noticing shop signs and so on. The simplest task can be used to 'expand horizons' and 'expose children to new learning'; it does not need to be anything out of the ordinary – it just requires reflective, open-minded staff who understand how tiny the world is for a 2-year-old and how they can open their world a tiny piece at a time.

On another occasion, the children were very hot, and a request for ice cream was made. This led to lots of discussions about the cost and counting the number of children and so on. Eventually, a visit to the manager in the office meant that there was some money available, and another trip to the shops was organised. Once the ice cream was purchased, the children sat in the shade to eat and listen to stories.

Quails eggs

One of the parents in the preschool room offered to bring in some quails' eggs that would hatch in the preschool. Since the preschool already had incubators, they welcomed this offer and the eggs arrived. The children from the toddler room were already used to visiting the preschool room and were fascinated to see these eggs and to watch them hatch over the period of a few days.

End of year trip

In the last few days of term, the weather suddenly changed and the rain was torrential. Unfortunately, this coincided with the end of year trip to Avon Valley Farm, but the weather did not spoil the experience for the families.

The journey continues

For some of the children in the toddler room, this is the end of their journey in this room, and they will move into the preschool room in September. For others, they will be here next year too. For all of them, the year has been a wonderful experience, and they have all become more resilient, confident, empathetic, communicative, independent, creative – the list goes on. For each child, the journey has been unique to suit their developmental path. The content of the play and the curriculum has emerged each day according to the interests of the children, but at every moment the well-being of the children has been prioritised and their levels of involvement have remained high, leading to outstanding progress in all areas of learning.

As this book goes to print, many of the children who appear in this book have moved into the preschool room with Shaneen. In October, I asked Shaneen how the first few weeks of the new term had been and if the settling period had been any different to previous years. This was the first year that the children had had a full year with the new systems in place in the 2–3 room, and I was interested to see how this had impacted on the children as they moved into the new room. Shaneen's comments were swift and definite:

> The children were far more independent, right from day one – happy to go off and explore and play independently. It was their personal, social and emotional development that is definitely higher than in previous years so that they are able to work and play together. They have settled so quickly – our first few weeks have been a dream!

The children have made excellent progress

The data from EExAT (see Chapter 5 for details) confirms what the staff and families already know. The children have made excellent progress in all areas of development. The screen shot from EExAT here shows this clearly too.

Early Excellence
Assessment Tracker

| Dashboard | Tracker | Evidence | Reports ▸ | Children | Moderation |

HC ▾

Some reports may take longer to load when processing large amounts of data.

Summary of Progress: toddler room september 2018 ⌄

This report compares the progress between the start of one window and the end of another, across all areas of learning.

The report can be used in conjunction with the Running Record Cumulative Score and shows the progress across a cohort or group as a bar chart.

You can click on each bar to find numbers, names and percentages of children making below typical, typical and above typical progress.

Use the filters to look at specific groups of children and the window tab to see progress for a previous year.

Please select the from and to windows

Window One - 2018/2019 ▸ to Window Three - 2018/2019 ▸

Filter by | Gender? ▸ | Pupil Premium? ▸ | SEND? ▸ | All Filters (2) | ▼ Clear Filters | ▼ Load Filter | Save Filter

Summary of Progress

	Below Typical Progress	Typical Progress	Above Typical Progress	Not Measured
	5% (1 child)	10% (2 children)	86% (18 children)	0% (0 children)

Hide Progress Guide Key ⟨⟩

Progress Guide	Below Typical Progress	Typical Progress	Above Typical Progress
In 4 months	< 14	14 - 16	> 16
In 8 months	< 28	28 - 32	> 32
In 12 months	< 42	42 - 48	> 48

Need help? ✉ tracking@earlyexcellence.com ✆ +44 (0)1422 311314

17 Conclusion

When I started writing this book, my granddaughter, Kayla, was nearly 2, and as I write this conclusion, she is about to turn 3. She remains happy, confident, resilient, empathetic, creative and curious. When I visit Staple Hill Stars Pre-school, I see children who are happy, confident, resilient, empathetic, creative and curious, and Kayla is one of those children. The preschool supports each unique child to thrive and to make outstanding progress in all areas of development. They do this by prioritising the well-being of the children, understanding that this is the essential prerequisite for all development. Without good well-being, a child cannot develop. With high well-being, the child is able to relax and engage with the environment, the people and the opportunities around them. The environment, the people and the opportunities are exactly suited to children of this age, ensuring that well-being and engagement are maximised, leading to maximum progress and development.

The staff understand that when a child is 'engaged', they are 'learning'.

And also when a child is 'not engaged', they are 'not learning'.

Through experience, they now know that the children are most deeply engaged (and therefore learning) when they have autonomy and choice – when they are in free-flow, child-initiated play. Therefore, the children have child-initiated play all day every day (with physical needs being met as needed).

I spoke to Helen Clegg, one of the owners of the preschool, to get her view on how the setting has developed in the last three years, and I would like to give her the final say in this conclusion. Three years ago, the preschool was run very differently. There were topics which changed each two weeks. Every area of the provision had pre-planned activities set up, and the resources were changed every fortnight as well. The day was highly structured and fragmented, with several interruptions and adult-led groups and tasks. There was no free-flow to outdoors and little autonomy or choice for the children. At the preschool now, the children arrive and have free-flow, child-initiated play from the moment they arrive. There are no interruptions and no pre-planned activities or topics. The role of the adults has had to change dramatically, and the staff have had to learn to follow the children rather than lead them. This journey of change has been exciting and challenging, and these are some of the comments from Helen:

"My main thought about this way of working is that the children can follow their own interests, and this means that they are more engaged and happy. The education system – as children go further up – seems very narrow, prescriptive and limiting. In the early years, we can allow children to follow their interests, strengths and passions, and therefore they remain enthusiastic when learning, exploring and developing. There is such a strong link between development, emotional well-being and engagement. If we get this right, every child will develop in their own unique way.

"We had to change our planning and we now plan 'in the moment'. When planning in the moment, you don't know where the learning will go. You have to think on your feet. The staff have to go to the children. They watch and wait to see what the child is doing and then they decide how to respond (by modelling, demonstrating, exploring ideas and so on) to move the learning on.

"We have had to make several changes to get to where we are now. The main change was in the role of the staff and getting them all to a point where they felt confident that this is the best approach for the children. We have a lot of visitors now, and I say to them (and to anyone reading this book) – take the leap and have a go. Some of our staff had reservations, but now they are all on board. They have been convinced by what has happened:

- The data shows that the children are making outstanding progress
- The atmosphere is purposeful and busy
- The behavior management has reduced massively
- The workload and paperwork has reduced too
- The staff feel that they really know all the children so much better

"Because the staff now know the children so well, they are able to move their learning on through their interactions. They know each child, what they are interested in, how they respond to adults and so on. This detailed knowledge ensures that their interactions are pitched uniquely to suit each child. Within their interactions, the staff had to get used to allowing the child to take the lead. They were no longer leading the play. They now go to the children, get down to their level, observe and then decide what to do. The children are leading and the adults are following.

"It also means that assessments are easy – staff say it is like assessing your own child. There is no need to look back at notes or observations; they just know the children, and so the assessments are accurate and quick to complete.

"The impact has been very noticeable:

- Progress is now greater
- The emotional well-being of the children is high
- The levels of engagement are high
- The atmosphere is calm and purposeful
- The children are happier and all the children are happy to be here

"My main message would be that settings should try this approach in its entirety. Have faith; child-initiated play, with planning in the moment, (*if* it is done well), will give results that will amaze you. It will also reignite your enthusiasm for early childhood education."

Appendix A: Levels of involvement

Ferre Laevers

Involvement focuses on the extent to which pupils are operating to their full capabilities. In particular it refers to whether the child is focused, engaged and interested in various activities.

The Leuven Scale for Involvement

1   Low Activity
    Activity at this level can be simple, stereotypic, repetitive and passive. The child is absent and displays no energy. There is an absence of cognitive demand. The child characteristically may stare into space. NB: This may be a sign of inner concentration.

2   A Frequently Interrupted Activity
    The child is engaged in an activity, but half of the observed period includes moments of non-activity in which the child is not concentrating and is staring into space. There may be frequent interruptions in the child's concentration, but his/her involvement is not enough to return to the activity.

3   Mainly Continuous Activity
    The child is busy at an activity, but it is at a routine level, and the real signals for involvement are missing. There is some progress but energy is lacking and concentration is at a routine level. The child can be easily distracted.

4   Continuous Activity with Intense Moments
    The child's activity has intense moments during which activities at Level 3 can come to have special meaning. Level 4 is reserved for the kind of activity seen in those intense moments and can be deduced from the 'involvement signals'. This level of activity is resumed after interruptions. Stimuli from the surrounding environment, however attractive, cannot seduce the child away from the activity.

5   Sustained Intense Activity
    The child shows continuous and intense activity revealing the greatest involvement. In the observed period, not all the signals for involvement need be there, but the essential ones must be present: concentration, creativity, energy and persistence. This intensity must be present for almost all the observation period.

Level of Involvement

Time	Involvement	Comments
Average		

Biscuits

🥄🥄🥄🥄 flour

🥄 sugar

🥄🥄 butter

Appendix C: Cake recipe book

Cake Recipe

You can use

1 egg or

2 eggs or 3 eggs or

4 eggs or 5 eggs or 6 eggs

More eggs = bigger cake!

Balance the eggs with the flour.

Put the flour in the bowl.

Balance the eggs with the sugar.

Put the sugar in the bowl.

Balance the eggs with the butter.

Put the butter in the bowl.

Add the eggs to the bowl.

Mix, mix, mix!

Put the mixture in a baking tray.

Cook at 180° C for 15 minutes.

Decorate your cake and eat it!

Appendix D: I am 2

Staple Hill Stars
Pre-School

'Learning to Play, Playing to Learn'

I Am Two: What Can I Do?

Name:

Date of Birth: Age in months:

Key Person:

My family have noticed that:	My Key Person has noticed that:	
How do I learn? Playing and Exploring:	**Personal, Social and Emotional**	
Active Learning:		
Creating and Thinking Critically:	Making Relationships	Self-confidence and Self-Awareness	Managing Feelings and Behaviour

Physical Development		Communication and Language		
Moving and Handling	Health and Self-care	Listening and Attention	Understanding	Speaking

Next Steps:

Comment from Child:

Parent/Carers_____ Key Person_____

Any other Contributor_____ Manager_____

Date form completed_____

One copy of this form to be kept in child's red Health Visitor book.

Appendix E: Focus child sheet

Staple Hill Stars Pre-School, Page Road, Staple Hill, Bristol, BS16 4NE
Telephone: 01179569888 Email: info@staplehillstars.co.uk

2018

Toddler Room

Dear Parent/Carer

At Staple Hill Stars Pre-school we really value the start you have given your children from tiny babies on their education journey. As the Early Years Foundation Stage states; 'Parents are children's first and most enduring educators. When parents and practitioners work together in early years settings, the results have a positive impact on children's learning and development.' It is known that what parents do at home with young children has the greatest impact on a child's social, emotional and intellectual development.

Each time your child comes to Pre-school our team spend time playing, listening, talking and facilitating learning through stimulating play based learning opportunities. Six times a year your child will be our focus child. During this week we all write down what your child is demonstrating he/she can do and what interests/learning was explored. During the interactions that are recorded we will write down the teaching and how each child's next steps are planned for in that moment and the learning that takes place. The adults will follow the child's lead as usually the good ideas for activities and learning opportunities come from the children themselves!

We would really like your contribution to this process. **Please use the form attached and return it to us by the date at the bottom.** We are always available to talk to and if you'd like to come and tell us in person we're more than happy to listen. We'd love you to email or send in some pictures which we can share with your child as part of this process.

Our email address is info@staplehillstars.co.uk

Please see your child's key worker to book in for a parent meeting appointment and to arrange a stay and play session to join your child for an hour during a session.

Thank you for your continued support,
The team at Staple Hill Stars Pre-school

Parent's Comments for Focus Week

Week beginning _____ we will be focusing on your child. We will be observing them while they play to find out more about their interests and how they are progressing. Please take some pictures (no more than 10) of your child enjoying activities out of preschool. Please email them to info@staplehillstars. co.uk. We value the knowledge and understanding you have of your child and would really appreciate it if you would share this with us so that we can work towards your child's learning and development together.

Name of Child:		Date	

Parent/Carer Comments:
You may wish to comment on . . .
What do they like to do/ play with at home?, The interactions/conversations they had with others during the observation.
Is there anything significant happening in your child's life at the moment e.g. visits, new pet, family celebrations?

Do you have anything you would like to ask about your child's progress and development?

Signed_____   date_____

Please return this sheet by_____
Please note that we do have one camera that we can loan out for a week if you are unable to take photos.
Please see your child's key worker to arrange an appointment to discuss your child and book in to stay and play with your child during a session.

Appendix F: Learning Journey

Learning Journey For .... Date ....

Entries should include the initial observation (& assessment), the teaching and the outcome.

Current interests, patterns in learning or information from parents

*
*
*

Possible Areas For Future Focus:

*

*

*

Appendix G: Learning Journey for a child with additional needs

Name-

Date-

Support Targets-

Observation, Teaching and Outcome

Wow Moments

Future Support Targets/ areas for development-

Appendix H: New Learning Journey

Learning Journey For .... Date ....

Entries should include the initial observation (& assessment), the teaching and the outcome.

Ideas for parents/carers to try at home:

*

*

*

Appendix I: Ofsted definition of teaching

"Teaching should not be taken to imply a 'top down' or formal way of working. It is a broad term that covers the many different ways in which adults help young children learn. It includes their interactions with children during planned and child-initiated play and activities: communicating and modelling language, showing, explaining, demonstrating, exploring ideas, encouraging, questioning, recalling, providing a narrative for what they are doing, facilitating and setting challenges. It takes account of the equipment adults provide and the attention given to the physical environment, as well as the structure and routines of the day that establish expectations."

Ofsted September 2019

Appendix J: Suppliers

www.creativecascade.co.uk – for Creative Cascade Sets and woodwork benches.

Skips, ditches, parents (great suppliers of 'junk modelling' resources), charity shops, etc.

DIY stores and online companies – for ropes, marine plywood, pulleys, woodwork tools and elasticated rope.

www.communityplaythings.co.uk – for wooden blocks (various sizes) and storage units.

www.costco.co.uk – for heavy duty tarpaulins and shelving.

www.cosydirect.com – for open-ended resources at reasonable prices.

www.ikea.co.uk – for storage units, canopies and children's furniture.

www.impbins.com – for salt bins.

www.olympicgymnasium.com – for A-Frames and ladders etc. Look in their 'nursery' section.

www.pvc-strip.co.uk – for plastic strips to hang in doorways.

www.shedstore.co.uk – for sheds (Model: Larchlap Overlap Maxi Wallstore 63 is useful for storing large wooden blocks).

www.earlyexcellence.com – for open shelving in particular.

www.filplastic.co.uk – for shopping baskets.

Appendix K: Play dough

You need:

1 cup of salt
2 cups of plain flour
4 teaspoons of cream of tartar
2 tablespoons of cooking oil
2 cups of boiling water
Food colouring
Large bowl

Mix all the ingredients in a large bowl.

If you keep the dough in a plastic bag or an airtight container, it will last about six weeks.

Bibliography

Athey, C. 1990. *Extending Thought in Young Children: A Parent-Teacher Partnership*. Paul Chapman Publishing Ltd. London.

Bilton, H. 2010. *Outdoor Learning in the Early Years*. Routledge. Oxfordshire.

Bowlby, J. 1997. *Attachment and Loss*. Pimlico. London.

Brooker, L. 2002. *Starting School*. Open University Press. Maidenhead.

Bruce, T. 1987. *Early Childhood Education*. 3rd Edition 2005. Hodder and Stoughton. London.

Bruce, T. 2001. *Learning Through Play: Babies, Toddlers and the Foundation Years*. Hodder Arnold. London.

Dyer, W. 2007. *Mercury's Child*. Booklocker.com, Inc. for Colly and Sons UK.

Ephgrave, A. 2012. *The Reception Year in Action*. 2nd Edition. Routledge. Oxfordshire.

Ephgrave, A. 2015. *The Nursery Year in Action*. Routledge. Oxfordshire.

Ephgrave, A. 2017. *Year One in Action*. Routledge. Oxfordshire.

Ephgrave, A. 2018. *Planning in the Moment with Young Children*. Routledge. Oxfordshire.

Fisher, J. 2002. *Starting from the Child*. 2nd Edition. Open University Press. Maidenhead.

Fisher, J. 2018. *Interacting or Interfering*. Open University Press. Maidenhead.

Gerhardt, S. 2004. *Why Love Matters*. Routledge. Hove.

Gray, P. 2013. *Free to Learn*. Basic Books. New York.

Greenfield, S. 2014. *Mind Change*. Rider. London.

Gussin-Paley, V. 1991. *The Boy Who Would Be a Helicopter*. Harvard University Press. Cambridge, MA.

Isaacs, S. 1929. *The Nursery Years*. Routledge & Kegan Paul. London.

Isaacs, S. 1966. *Intellectual Growth in Young Children*. Shockern Books. New York.

Laevers, F. 1994. *Five Levels of Well-Being*. Leuven University Press. Leuven, Belgium.

Legerstee, M., Haley, D., & Bornstein, M. 2013. *The Infant Mind*. The Guilford Press. New York.

Moorhouse, P. 2018. *Learning Through Woodwork*. Routledge. Oxfordshire.

Nutbrown, C. 2006. *Threads of Thinking*. 3rd Edition. Sage. London.

Passy, J. 2010. *Cued Articulation*. STASS Publications. St. Mabyn, Cornwall.

Pellegrini, A.D. 2011. *The Oxford Handbook of the Development of Play*. Oxford University Press. Oxford.

Read, V., & Hughes, A. 2009. *Developing Attachment in Early Years Settings*. David Fulton Publishers. Oxfordshire.

Robinson, D., & Groves, J. 2002. *Introducing Bertrand Russell*. Icon Books. Cambridge.

Robinson, K., & Aronica, L. 2015. *Creative Schools*. Viking Penguin. New York.

Rose, S., & Rogers, J. 2012. *The Role of the Adult in Early Years*. Open University Press. Maidenhead.

Russell, D. 1932. *In Defence of Children*. Hamish Hamilton. London.

Solly, K. 2014. *Risk, Challenge and Adventure in the Early Years*. Routledge. Oxfordshire.

Strutt, S. 2019. *Inspiring Learning Through Cooking*. Routledge. Oxfordshire.

Vygotsky, L.S. 1987. *Mind in Society*. Harvard University Press. Cambridge, MA.

Whalley, M. 2007. *Involving Parents in their Children's Learning*. 2nd Edition. Paul Chapman Publishing. London.

Index

For training and/or consultancy work with Anna Ephgrave, please email enquiries@creativecascade.co.uk